MW00532013

...AFTERWORDS

A COOL CUSTOMER

Joan Didion's
The Year of Magical Thinking

Jacob Bacharach

FICTION ADVOCATE
New York • San Francisco • Providence

A Fiction Advocate Book

A Cool Customer:
Joan Didion's *The Year of Magical Thinking*
© 2018 by Jacob Bacharach
All Rights Reserved

ISBN: 978-0-9899615-8-5

No part of this book may be reproduced, stored in a retrieval system, or transmitted by any means without the written permission of the author and publisher.

FICTION ADVOCATE
New York • San Francisco • Providence
fictionadvocate.com

Published in the United States of America

CONTENTS

CHAPTER 1

MAGICAL THINKING

The hardest part of writing about Didion is trying not to sound like her. Right now, I am trying to reconstruct the date and time—the moment—when I first read *The Year of Magical Thinking*. I am having trouble, and the uncertainty of the reconstruction is making me sound in my own ear like Joan Didion. I am reading through the correspondence I sent at the time—for example, emails to an ex-boyfriend with whom I was unadvisedly getting back together. I had remembered being single when I first read *The Year of Magical Thinking*, but there is the evidence in my inbox; there he is, calling me "honey" in a note about picking something up for him at the store. There are also, in those emails, that certain frisson between two people about to make the same mistake all over again. I am reading through other emails to my friend Heather, who was at the time a curator at the Albright–Knox Gallery in Buffalo, New York, to see if I can find some mention of the visit I made in what must have been the late fall or early winter of 2009. *The Year of Magical Thinking* came out in 2005, but I was never an especially timely reader. Now that I'm a writer, a novelist, I'm critical of this part of my character; I should be better about reading books when they first appear. But with *The Year of Magical Thinking*, I waited. And the thing is, I didn't even start by reading it. I started by listening to it, or the first few hours of it anyway, on a drive from Pittsburgh to Buffalo to visit my friend Heather the year my younger brother died.

So for me, the act of reviewing this book by Joan Didion, perhaps her most celebrated in a long and generally celebrated writing life, is not just an effort to avoid the sort of pastiche that a decent writer tries to avoid when writing about a much better one. It is also a project of autobiography, one step farther along the dangerous path of authorial imitation, because my first encounters with the book that is the subject of this long review so closely correspond with a period in my life in which I, too, was engaged in some deep pretending, imagining that, among other things, there might be some kind of cure for what I felt.

I must have been just barely out of Pittsburgh when I got to this passage: "'He's dead, isn't he?' I heard myself say to the doctor. The doctor looked at the social worker. 'It's okay,' the social worker said. 'She's a pretty cool customer.'" I'd thought of myself as a pretty cool customer, too. I'd only cried once, really, in secret so my mother wouldn't see or hear me, when I was in the basement of my parents' house in Uniontown writing my brother's obituary, which neither my mother nor my father could bear to do.

"The question of self-pity," Didion wrote. They were among "the first words I wrote after it happened." But it isn't quite true; that isn't quite the question. She is, as she'd said in *Where I Was From*, coming at it "obliquely." The question is how to understand, amid the universality of death and sickness, the incredible peculiarity of *each* death and *each* sickness, and how then to reconstruct a general model of grief from the terrible and unrepeatable particulars. I intend to try to understand how *The Year of Magical Thinking* builds that model. There is a scene in the book, a memory, where John Gregory Dunne, Didion's now late husband, stands in a swimming pool rereading *Sophie's Choice* to figure out "how it worked." I intend to reread *The Year of Magical Thinking* to figure out how it works.

CHAPTER 2

SADNESS AND HAPPINESS

That they have no earthly measure
is well known—the surprise is
how often it becomes impossible
to tell one from the other in memory...

—ROBERT PINSKY, "Sadness And Happiness"

I came to appreciate Joan Didion because I found a person who was very much like me, although that idea is superficially absurd. Didion isn't quite of my grandparents' generation, but she's very much of the generation preceding my parents'; they were only fifteen when *Slouching Towards Bethlehem* came out. She's a slight, painfully shy, lapsed Episcopalian Californian of pioneer stock, and I'm a loud, gangly Easterner (or Midwesterner—wherever you want to place Pittsburgh, which is neither exactly the one nor the other) just a few generations down the line from a bunch of Ukrainian Jewish and Italian Catholic immigrants. I found, nevertheless, a reflection in her habits of skepticism, in the way she came at the proper opinions that people of good backgrounds and good education are supposed to hold, in the way this famously shy woman unashamedly made herself, like Montaigne, the subject matter of her own books, whatever their ostensible topics. I found someone who seemed at once conservative and anarchic in her ideological affiliations. I found a "cool customer."

But the truth is complicated. I had actively avoided *The Year of Magical Thinking.* I was in my twenties then. The Didion I wanted to read was writing slim conspiracy novels about Iran-Contra. She was writing about how Reagan compared the presidency to a day on a movie set. She was being mean to Bob Woodward. She was skewering the self-involvement and grandiosity and delusions of her and my parents' generations, who had, in the intervening years leading to my own new adulthood, really royally fucked everything up for the rest of us: bequeathed to us a dry-drunk Bush *fils* and Dick Cheney and climate change and the Iraq War and student debt and Enron and the mujahideen and the Saudis who destroyed the World Trade Center.

I wasn't especially interested in grief, and I wasn't especially interested in reading the memoir of an old woman who'd lost her husband. It seemed like the sort of book for your mother's book club.

There's an irony in this, because one of the repeated observations of *The Year of Magical Thinking* is the way that our image of ourselves and our image of the others in our lives become fixed, how jarring it is when, through force of circumstance, we're forced to look at how far the present reality has drifted from the fixed reference point of the past. Didion's daughter, Quintana Roo, is always a girl, barefoot, in a dress—even when she gets married, she remains in a sense that girl—until suddenly she is not: cracked, swollen, intubated in an induced coma in this hospital or that. Didion writes:

> Marriage is not only time: it is also, paradoxically, the denial of time. For forty years I saw myself through John's eyes. I did not age. This year for the first time since I was twenty-nine I saw myself through the eyes of others. This year for the first time since I was twenty-nine I realized that my image of myself was of someone significantly younger. This year I realized that one reason I was so often sideswiped by memories of Quintana at

three was this: when Quintana was three I was thirty-four.

It's no exaggeration to say that many of us likewise prefer to recall the particular writers we love in a similar way. Amber. There is a proprietary impulse toward certain memories that anchors them to a particular time and tries to deny them the right to drift too far away. Who wants to read about a woman he admires becoming fragile, demented, old?

In fact, this is a bit of a theme in the reviews. "I need to explain here that *The Year of Magical Thinking* is not a downer. On the contrary," Robert Pinsky says in his *New York Times* review. He goes on to compare the book to an adventure story, "a forced expedition into those 'cliffs of fall' identified by Hopkins." I won't deny that there's some truth in this assessment; on the other hand, it has the insistent ding of a salesman peddling a health product. *Yes, it's good for you, but it's also* delicious. The truth is that *The Year of Magical Thinking* is indeed a bit of a downer, and while I appreciate what Pinsky was trying to do—a positive book review, after all, *is* a kind of a sales pitch; particularly in an outlet like the *Times*, it's hard to separate the review from its function in a system of economic exchange—I also find it a little disingenuous. This book is many things, but it is an *adventure* story only if you accept the adventure as the most ductile of comparisons, stretched to an angel-hair filament.

The reviews of *The Year of Magical Thinking* were, it's no stretch to say, largely rapturous, and this gives many of them this shared quality of a slight disingenuousness. "Didion is ultimately less like a camera than a precise seismograph," Pinsky writes. This metaphor is more apt, if accidentally. In her essay "In the Islands," which Didion remembers in *The Year of Magical Thinking*, she describes herself and Dunne as having landed on "this island in the middle of the Pacific in lieu of filing for divorce." She and Dunne and Quintana Roo, a fixed image at three years old in a "frangipani lei," are stuck inside because "[t]here has been an earthquake in the Aleutians, 7.5 on the Richter scale, and a tidal wave is expected." The tidal wave never comes. "In the absence of a natural disaster we are left again to our own uneasy devices."

In its prepublication review of *The Year of Magical Thinking*, *Kirkus* is ambivalent: "But perhaps because it is a work of such intense personal emotion, this memoir lacks the mordant bite of her earlier work." The reading public doesn't pay any attention to *Kirkus* unless a glowing review is excerpted as a blurb, and those of us who write books and actually do pay attention to prepub reviews know that it prefers to swim smirkingly against the tide of any potentially emerging consensus, but I still find something authentic about its offhanded semidismissal. "A potent depiction of grief, but also a book lacking the originality and acerbic prose that distinguished Didion's earlier writing." I think this judgment is wrong; I think its confusion of acerbity with exactness is a serious critical error. But the *Kirkus* review captures some of my own initial reluctance to read and engage *The Year of Magical Thinking*. "This latest work concentrates almost entirely on the author's personal suffering and confusion—even her husband and daughter make but fleeting appearances—without connecting them to the larger public delusions that have been her special terrain." Her "personal suffering and confusion." I was twenty-four in October of 2005 when *The Year of Magical Thinking* was published.

CHAPTER 3

WHERE SHE WAS FROM

At some point, in the interest of remembering what seemed most striking about what had happened, I considered adding those words, "the ordinary instant." I saw immediately that there would be no need to add the word "ordinary," because there would be no forgetting it: the word never left my mind. It was in fact the ordinary nature of everything preceding the event that prevented me from truly believing it had happened, absorbing it, incorporating it, getting past it. I recognize now that there was nothing unusual in this: confronted with sudden disaster we all focus on how unremarkable the circumstances were in which the unthinkable occurred, the clear blue sky from which the plane fell, the routine errand that ended on the shoulder with the car in flames, the swings where the children were playing as usual when the rattle-snake struck from the ivy.

—Joan Didion, *The Year of Magical Thinking*

Something that struck me in Pinsky's review was a passing mention of Didion's having reported on "the vanishing of an old provincial California." It's in the context of a list of the many topical interests of her essays, and yet it struck me, because the book she wrote immediately prior to *The Year of Magical Thinking* was *Where I Was From*, a memoir and historiography that looked back and smashed to bits any idea that there ever had been "an old provincial California" that could vanish. In *Where I Was From*, Didion turns the "originality and acerbic prose" that *Kirkus* so admired onto her own participation in that myth. "You were meant, if you were a Californian, to know how to lash together a corral with bark, you were meant to know how to tent a raft and live on the river, you were meant to show spirit, kill the rattlesnake, keep moving." Didion's own grandfather had been insistent on the point about the snake. If you see a rattlesnake, you kill it. And yet, Didion recalls vividly an episode in which she saw a rattlesnake on a playground and did not.

The idea of catastrophe emerging from the "ordinary instant" recurs throughout *The Year of Magical Thinking*, but so too does it slowly emerge that *catastrophe* itself is ordinary, mundane. The tension between this idea of death as a part of the background texture of the ordinary versus death as an emergent and particular phenomenon forms one of the central organizing principles of the book. Among the bibliography of the literature of death and dying that Didion consulted, Philippe Ariès's *Western Attitudes toward Death* figures prominently, and in the middle of that collected series of lectures, he considers precisely that tension:

> In the past death in bed was a solemn event, but also an event as banal as seasonal holidays. People expected it, and when it occurred they followed the rituals laid down by custom. But in the nineteenth century, a new passion stirred those present. Emotion shook them. They cried, prayed, gesticulated. They did not refuse to go through the activities dictated by custom; on the contrary. But while performing them, they stripped them of their banal and customary character. Henceforth these activities were described as if they had been invented for the first time, spontaneously, inspired by a passionate sorrow which is unique among sorrows.

It's worth noting that Ariès's work subsequently came in for some sharp criticism for its cultural and geographic specificity. Some contended that his relatively neat taxonomy of old attitudes and new flattened a more complex history, that you could find, if you looked, equal counterexamples of new attitudes way back when and old attitudes persisting into the present day. But the distinctions he draws between the behavior of people for whom death is ordinary and those for whom it's extraordinary are still worthwhile. "Certainly, the expression of sorrow by survivors is owing to a new intolerance of separation," he goes on to say. Didion says, "Husbands walk out, wives walk out, divorces happen, but these husbands and wives leave behind them webs of intact associations, however acrimonious. Only the survivors of death are truly left alone."

The Episcopalian graveside liturgy says, "In the midst of life we are in death." Didion mentions this almost immediately in *The Year of Magical Thinking*.

It's striking that she mentions this same passage in *Where I Was From*, a book whose final section is about the death, in 2001, of Didion's mother, who was both an exemplar and a victim of the California mythology Didion was dissecting. In fact, I found, in rereading that book, a surprising continuity with *Magical Thinking*. It might be fair to say that even prior to Quintana's sudden critical illness and John Dunne's seemingly more sudden death, Didion was a writer for whom the topic of age and mortality were already a prominent concern.

In his *London Review of Books* review, Michael Wood notes this sense of continuity:

> Didion's cool gaze picks up contradictions everywhere but she also realizes that the contradictions are the point, precisely what the myth both denies and thrives on. Her word here is "muddle" rather than "magic" (although she does call herself muddled in *The Year of Magical Thinking* too). And she wants to step free of the muddle, as the odd tense of her title suggests (is it even idiomatic to ask someone where she "was" from?).

This is a strong passage in a review that otherwise reads mostly like a book report, a noticeably common problem in the reviews of *Magical Thinking*. I don't think this is because these are bad reviewers necessarily, but rather because, from a writer known for a certain kind of opacity, *Magical Thinking* has very little to strip away, judge, explicate, elaborate. When she's ready, she says what she means. One of the premises, or conventions, of the review and the critical essay as genres is that a book is a motor whose interworking parts, whose mechanism, can be explained. But Didion was always insistent that stories are things imposed on lives. *The Year of Magical Thinking* is all the more remarkable as a work of autobiography in that it resists so tenaciously the urge to make itself into a story.

"Biography," says the character of Oscar Wilde in Tom Stoppard's 1997 play *The Invention of Love*, "is the mesh through which our real life escapes." It is probably worth noting that the play takes place largely in the underworld.

CHAPTER 4

A PUBLIC TO A PRIVATE RITUAL

As of this writing, there have only been two significant deaths in my close family for as long as I've been alive: my paternal grandfather, Fritz, in 2004 at eighty-four years old, and my brother, Nathan, five years later. He'd just turned twenty-six. I'll say more about Nate later. He is in many ways the reason I wrote any of this at all. But I need to work up to it, so let me first say a few things about my grandfather instead.

Fritz—we only ever called him Fritz—had fought in World War II in the Pacific, driven a bread delivery truck, and, since 1956, owned a bar on Penn Avenue in Pittsburgh called the Evergreen Cafe. The bar is still owned by my uncle Phil, the youngest of the five boys Fritz had with my grandmother, Lena. We only ever call her Lena. They owned a cottage on a creek near Ligonier, and my image of him, which persists even now, is of a skinny sixtysomething man with thick gray hair and Popeye's weirdly muscled forearms, sitting on the swing in the yard in a white T-shirt, drinking a Rolling Rock and smoking a cigarette. This has to be an early memory, because Fritz quit smoking after his first bypass operation, and by the time I was a teenager he'd become notably frail. He was a quiet and stoical man; he was funny, although in keeping with his character, he only ever delivered a joke in a deadpan. I saw a picture of myself taken recently on a friend's back porch. I am sitting on a glider, and my own slightly out-of-proportion forearms are crossed over my skinny chest, and I look for all the world like an image of my grandfather.

In *Where I Was From*, Didion tells this story about her mother, which startled me because it reminded me so uncannily of my paternal grandparents:

> Yet she had herself at age twelve refused outright to be confirmed an Episcopalian: she had gone through the instruction and been presented to the bishop, but, when asked for the usual rote affirmation of a fairly key doctrinal point, had declared resoundingly, as if it were a debate, that she found herself "incapable of believing" that

Christ was the son of God. By the time of my
own confirmation, she had further hardened this
position. "The only church I could possibly go to
would be Unitarian," she announced when my
grandmother asked why she never went to church
with us.

Lena once told me that her marriage to Fritz was
slightly unusual at the time, a mixed marriage really,
since he was a German Jew and she an Italian Catholic. "But I always tell people that your grandfather
married the only Italian woman who can't cook, and I
married the only Jew with no money." In fact, neither
of them was religious. Lena's father was a putterer
and failed inventor who wanted to invent a perpetual
motion machine. Fritz's father left Orthodox Judaism
for the new Reform movement, found it too dogmatic,
and became a Unitarian, but soon quit that as well.
Fritz's family was so irreligious that no one immediately noticed that when his brother, my great-uncle,
was buried in Arlington National Cemetery, they put
a cross rather than a Star of David on his headstone.

If a picture of Fritz from my childhood persists,
I nevertheless remember him more distinctly in the
poor health of his later years. He had congestive heart

failure among other accumulative maladies, and in the last few years we had to install a lift on the staircase of my grandparents' house so that he could get to the bedroom and bath. On one of his last stints in Shadyside Hospital—perhaps it was his last—he indicated the ceiling of his room and told Lena, "That's me up there." One of the few times I've ever seen her visibly upset—she is as stoical as her late husband—was when she told us that story.

I think of Fritz's death when Didion cites Ariès in *The Year of Magical Thinking,* because the historical turn he identifies, the change of death from a public to a private ritual, was not the case in my family. Fritz didn't want to die in a hospital; we didn't want him to die there. My father and uncles arranged for him to come home. He spent his last days in a bed in the living room on Reynolds Street. The uncles sat with him, as did the aunts, the grandkids, the old friends from the neighborhood. He was in pain, but there were drugs for that. He smoked a cigarette, the first smoke he'd had in a decade, probably. He died at night. The H. Samson Funeral Home on Neville Street is no longer there; it was torn down not long after we received visitors there to make way for a reflective complex of pricey condominiums, an early indicator of Pittsburgh's coming boom. The same people who'd visited him at the house came to the funeral. I remember at one point the staff had to come and ask us to keep it down. All that laughing was disturbing another visitation.

I also think of Fritz and of my family—all the aunts and uncles and cousins and second cousins and not-quite-sure-but-we're-related types—when I think about the affinity I feel for Didion's own self-identification as a conservative who isn't a conservative. I had once described my own politics as conservative anarchism; I'm a queer writer who wants to smash the empire but who feels an abiding sense of the inherent, irreplaceable value of a multigenerational family. There's a contradiction here, but it feels like a necessary one, like the ardent Goldwater gal who later learned that politics is fiction.

One of the things I am trying to understand is what it is that makes a person fall in love with a book, with an author. What tips a reader from liking a sentence, an essay, a novel, into trying to read everything that a writer has written. The myth of creative genius in our culture tends to focus the attention on the author; the work exists independently, and we either appreciate it or do not, *get it* or don't. But I tend to think that the affection we feel for art, especially for literature, which

is so human because it *speaks*, is very much like the
affection we feel for other people—for our friends, for
instance. I think we can all admit that there are plenty
of fine people in the world, plenty of great people we've
actually met, with whom we never hit it off. We never
become friends; we become acquainted. We meet once
and forget each other. And there are plenty of excellent
books about which we can say the same. We read them,
we enjoy them, we admire them. We don't love them.

To love a book is to find yourself in conversation
with it, to have, in a sense, a relationship with it: a kind
of friendship, a sort of affair. It would be easy enough to
say that I happened to encounter Didion's essay collec-
tion *Political Fictions* at just the right time for a young
political wacko to encounter *Political Fictions*; that I
happened to read her novel *The Last Thing He Wanted*
just when I was getting interested in conspiracy narra-
tives; that I listened to *The Year of Magical Thinking*
right after my twenty-six-year-old brother died—my
brother who was my best friend, my brother who told
me when he was only fourteen, a freshman in high
school, that I shouldn't worry about kids making fun
of him because his brother was the one out gay kid in
the school (something he'd heard my mother and me
discussing)—and that I was therefore primed to form
a sentimental but superficial attachment to the book.

The fact is that I find, as I think through all the times I've read it, a series of more complicated connections, a kind of genealogy of interests and attitudes. Let me revise something I wrote earlier. I'm not just interested in figuring out how *The Year of Magical Thinking* works. I'm interested in figuring out how it works *on me*.

CHAPTER 6

THE CENTRAL FACT OF THE SITUATION

One of the weirder things about the death of a close loved one is the expectation that the immediate bereaved become biographers and correspondents. Maybe this is a holdover from the lost public death that Ariès reflects on; because the friends, neighbors, acquaintances, colleagues, distant relatives are not literally in the room when the person dies, there is some obligation for those who were, or who nearly were, to describe the death so that the others can imagine they were there too. But is the eyewitness really the most suited to the job? Didion gets quickly to the heart of it:

> "And then—gone." *In the midst of life we are in death*, Episcopalians say at the graveside. Later I realized that I must have repeated the details of what happened to everyone who came to the

house in those first weeks, all those friends and relatives who brought food and made drinks and laid out plates on the dining room table for however many people were around at lunch or dinner time, all those who picked up the plates and froze the leftovers and ran the dishwasher and filled our (I could not yet think *my*) otherwise empty house even after I had gone into the bedroom (our bedroom, the one in which there still lay on a sofa a faded terrycloth XL robe bought in the 1970s at Richard Carroll in Beverly Hills) and shut the door. Those moments when I was abruptly overtaken by exhaustion are what I remember most clearly about the first days and weeks. I have no memory of telling anyone the details, but I must have done so, because everyone seemed to know them. At one point I considered the possibility that they had picked up the details of the story from one another, but immediately rejected it: the story they had was in each instance too accurate to have been passed from hand to hand. It had come from me.

On the next page, she reflects, however, on her problem putting the story together. She had failed in her initial attempt to explain what had happened to their housekeeper, José, who had to clean the blood from where Dunne had fallen after his heart attack. The syringes and other detritus of the EMTs Didion could handle herself, but not the blood. "When I first told him what had happened he had not understood," she writes. "Clearly I was not the ideal teller of this story, something about my version had been at once too offhand and too elliptical, something in my tone had failed to convey the central fact of the situation."

"The way I write is who I am, or have become," Didion reflects, quietly echoing something long held as the principal criticism of her writing—that it, and she, are *all* style. And yet she wishes she had "instead of words and rhythms a cutting room." She needs "more than words to find the meaning." She wants "whatever it is I think or believe to be penetrable."

In an interview with Hilton Als in the *Paris Review*, several years after *The Year of Magical Thinking* was published, during a period when she was adapting it as a one-woman play, Didion says of her political writing, "If I am sufficiently interested in a political situation to write a piece about it, I generally have a point of view, although I don't usually recognize it. Something about a situation will bother me, so I will write a piece to find out what it is that bothers me."

It strikes me that, while "bothers me" may be an unduly anodyne way to describe the grief you feel when a spouse of forty years dies and your grown but still young child is in and out of critical care for a series of mysterious and complex illnesses, it is nevertheless a pretty neat description of how *The Year of Magical Thinking* introduces itself and its methods. We enter the book *not* at the moment of Dunne's death, though we get there within a few pages, but rather, at the moment that Didion began to write it, a precise date looking back at a precisely timestamped file, neither of them the actual *event* itself.

And even in the second chapter, in the middle of describing in greater and more obviously journalistic narrative detail the moment when Dunne, just before dinner, slumped to the table and then fell dead to the floor, the victim of a "cardiac event" (as I've heard doctors refer to these things when they're not yet sure which cardiac event, precisely, it is), there remains a certain futility, a kind of impotence, in the attempt to put it into words. "When the paramedics came I tried to tell them what happened," she writes, but they brush her aside and set about doing what paramedics do. Of course, on the most obvious and practical level, this has nothing to do with the inadequacy of Didion's attempts to narrate the story. On a practical level, these are just professionals rushing past to get to work as quickly as possible in a critical and acute medical emergency. But there is yet the sense that another part of the problem *is* in the telling. "Life changes fast" is the first line of the book. And a book is a long, slow thing. So how is a writer to render on a page the way the brief moments of crisis expand and the way the long recoveries afterward collapse in on themselves?

CHAPTER 6

LITERALLY

On the other hand, *The Year of Magical Thinking* is very much a corrective to the contemporary view of death as a kind of catastrophe, as a crisis. A note I made to myself in the margins of page 188 of my paperback copy, the first page of chapter seventeen: "A function of its particularity, maybe—except as a *whole book*—can it really be described—explained." I didn't use a question mark. I am slightly embarrassed, actually, of my marginalia, which, when I go back to it, has an uncanny similarity to the slightly batty social-media eructations of Joyce Carol Oates. But I do think there's a point lurking in there, however silly the phrasing. "Grief turns out to be a place none of us know until we reach it" is the first sentence on the page.

I remember being immediately thunderstruck when I read Jonathan Yardley's *Washington Post* review of *The*

Year of Magical Thinking, which declares in the second paragraph that "[i]t is an intensely personal story that involves a relatively small cast of characters, but Didion's telling of it is clearly impelled in large measure by the events in New York of September 2001."

It struck me as wrong on a couple of levels. First: it is *full* of characters, though many of them flash by. In one passage in chapter five, at Didion and Dunne's wedding, we encounter Didion's mother, Dunne's brothers, his brother's wife Lenny and their four-year-old daughter, a gaggle of Didion's other close and distant family, Dunne's Princeton roommate, Quintana's cousins, her husband Gerry, some of his family, Otto Preminger, Barry Farrell and his wife Marcia, Katharine Ross, Conrad Ross, Jean and Brian Moore, Conrad's sister Nancy, and Earl McGrath. Elsewhere in the book are doctors—like the young doctor who calls Didion a "cool customer" at the hospital—and social workers and paramedics and pilots, agents and editors, old friends and acquaintances. On and on. Now you might argue that these are not really characters, that those named and unnamed people that flash by in chapter five are closer to setting than character.

You wouldn't be wrong, exactly, but I am looking at another note I made in the margins. "Your Aunt

Marty," it says. I'm talking about my Aunt Marty, although I could be talking about most of my aunts and uncles and certainly my grandmother Lena, who all have a habit of telling stories peopled with characters from the extended family or from the couple of streets in the neighborhood of Point Breeze, in Pittsburgh, where most of them have lived for the better part of five decades. The thing to mention here is that because my father's work had moved us when my brother and I were just kids to a couple of other towns outside of the city, neither we nor my mother knew most of these people, or, if we did, we only vaguely recognized a first name or a nickname—often from some *other* story. It isn't exclusionary or deliberately obscure to mention these first names or nicknames in passing as part of ordinary conversation in a large but close family whose conversations often consist of a kind of rambling storytelling. On the contrary, it's a signal of intimacy. It is an assumption of shared experience. It represents a taking into confidence. Didion has occasionally been accused of name-dropping: people, stores, hotels, restaurants. It is sometimes taken as a careless class marker and a further indication of a woman whose writing is more texture and surface than depth, but I find that the habit—and it *is* a habit in her writing—is instead a mark of familiarity, a way of bringing a reader into the writer's close circle, even if you're not sure, exactly, who or what or where some of these people or hotels or restaurants are.

The sillier idea in that Yardley quotation, however, is the idea that *Magical Thinking* was impelled by the "events in New York of September 2001." This is, first of all, a remarkably affected locution. By 2005, when the book appeared and the review was written, "9/11" was well settled in the common lexicon as the proper name for those "events in New York." More pointedly, it widely misses its critical target, which, over two hundred odd pages, seeks among other things to dispel any notion of death, of grief, as a set of fixed rituals and generic, universal meanings. "We do not look beyond the few days or weeks that follow such an imagined death." "We do not expect to be literally crazy."

In fact, the topic of literal craziness is central to another contemporaneous Didion work, which is her lecture-turned-essay "Fixed Opinions, or The Hinge of History," on the eponymous fixed opinions of America after 9/11. In it, she specifically indicts the permanent political class for hijacking the dislocation of national mourning to long-simmering and frankly nefarious ends. If, in any case, *The Year of Magical Thinking* returns recursively to the scene of John Dunne's death and the scene (scenes, really) of an unconscious Quintana's hospital bedside, then it is not in order to fondle the "events," but rather to drive home the endless outward ripple of these small pebbles on the wider water.

In the version of grief we imagine, the model will be "healing." A certain forward movement will prevail. The worst days will be the earliest days. We imagine that the moment to most severely test us will be the funeral, after which this hypothetical healing will take place. When we anticipate the funeral we wonder about failing to "get through it," rise to the occasion, exhibit the "strength" that invariably gets mentioned as the correct response to death. We anticipate needing to steel ourselves for the moment: will I be able to greet people, will I be able to leave the scene, will I be able even to get dressed that day? We have no way of knowing that this will not be the issue. We have no way of knowing that the funeral itself will be anodyne, a kind of narcotic regression in which we are wrapped in the care of others and the gravity and meaning of the occasion. Nor can we know ahead of the fact (and here lies the heart of the difference between grief as we imagine it and grief as it is) the unending absence that follows, the void, the very opposite of meaning, the relentless succession of moments during which we will confront the experience of meaninglessness itself.

What we imagine to be an event, a moment, turns out to be something closer to duration, to a condition. In that way, it recalls the question of character versus setting above; it calls for a kind of description without narrative. "We tell ourselves stories in order to live," Didion wrote, probably her most famous single line, the line that became the title of her collected non-fiction prior to *Magical Thinking*. It's hard not to find your eye lingering a little more on the word *stories*. It's hard not to feel a knot at the word *live*.

CHAPTER 7

THE RAMBAM

Didion has always used a combination of repetition and varying lengths of line, sentence, and paragraph to achieve the rhythmic effects for which her prose is known and praised. Interestingly, for a writer so thoroughly associated with her prose, these are techniques associated with modern poetry. Worth noting: in the American poetic tradition, there is a direct line connecting the methods of free verse, through Whitman, to the anaphoric rhythms of the Old Testament. Didion uses these tools frequently and heavily in *The Year of Magical Thinking*, and—probably not by accident—this gives much of the book an incantatory and liturgical feeling.

One of the pieces of common praise in almost every review notes her deep delve into the literature of death and grief—however crazy she may be in the year after Dunne's death, she is still a journalist, still a researcher. But I also note that she occasionally has a journalist's habit of skimming for the pull quote, of finding what she wants in the first quarter of the source material and setting it aside to get on with her own writing. (Incidentally, this is something you also note in book reviews when you begin writing them and therefore begin paying closer attention to the way they're written; it's actually quite shocking how often a reviewer seems to have stopped at the halfway mark.) For example, when she quotes Ariès's *The Hour of Our Death*, the quotations are from the first couple of pages. Which is a habit, also, of eulogists.

What interests her in Ariès is an account of the dying man's premonition of his own death. "I tell you that I shall not live two days," she quotes Ariès quoting Gawain from *La Chanson de Roland*. She is haunted, almost hunted, throughout her own book by a doubled dread that John had anticipated his own death and that she *ought to have* anticipated it as well. ("The mind possesses and is possessed by all the ruins / Of every haunted, hunted generation's celebration." —Delmore Schwartz, "Narcissus.") John had a pacemaker. He had a history of heart problems. On page twenty-three, he asks her to write a note in her notebook for him, because he'd forgotten his own note cards. She does, but "[w]hen I gave him the note the next day, he said, 'You can use it if you want to.'"

What did he mean?

Did he know he would not write the book?

Did he have some apprehension, a shadow? Why had he forgotten to bring note cards to dinner that night? Had he not warned me when I forgot my own notebook that the ability to make a note when something came to mind was the difference between being able to write and not being able to write? Was something telling him that night that the time for being able to write was running out?

John Dunne's father had died in his early fifties of a heart attack. Didion worries that she should have carried it as a warning. Much later in the book, she reveals that Dunne had, in fact, been warning her for years: "*When something happens to me*, he would frequently say." Of course, she'd reply that nothing was going to happen to him.

Despite all the precision of her writing and her recollections, and despite all the times I've read and reread this book, I'm still not sure how much of this is the banal and utterly commonplace backward projection of survivor's guilt and how much of it is more acutely and particularly a detail of Dunne's actual life and death. I'm not sure Didion knows either. Except in those cases where the dead really do give us fair warning—when Gawain announces his own end, when my grandfather comes home from the hospital to smoke a last cigarette and drink a last whiskey and die in his own living room—there is, I think, a universal sense that we should have seen it coming. This, in turn, is the sense that, having seen it coming, we might somehow have turned the wheel and avoided the cliff. That is to say, this kind of thinking—it is one of the varieties of the magical thinking that Didion is writing about—is the false idea that mortality is something we can control, that *someone else's* mortality is something we can control. Didion admits to a kind of obsession, even as Dunne was in an ambulance on the way to the hospital, dead but not yet *officially* dead, with performing in a way that would demonstrate to John that she was "handling" things.

When my brother died, I remember two simultaneous and overwhelming sensations. "Sensations" is the wrong word. "Imperatives" is probably better. The first was simple and possible. I had to get back to

Uniontown; I had to get to my parents' house. I was at work, and my dad had called me on my cell phone. I'd been in a meeting, or I'd been on another call, and I hadn't picked up the first time. He called me again immediately, and I knew, even before I answered. But I did answer, and he told me my brother was "gone." We were never a family that used a lot of circumlocution. No one ever said that Fritz had "passed." Fritz had died. But my brother was only twenty-six. My brother was, in all of our eyes, probably unrealistically, probably incorrectly, still basically a boy.

The second thing I felt was that I had to do something about it, as I had been trying to *do something* about Nathan for the last couple of years. Nate was an opiate addict. He'd broken his leg very badly playing a pickup game of soccer in college, before he'd dropped out of college. They had to put in a metal rod. He was prescribed painkillers, which he never stopped using for the rest of his life, until near the end when, strapped for cash and out of scripts, he turned to heroin. He was, as many addicts are, immensely charming. He was funny and good-looking. He worked in a hair salon and as a bartender. He excelled at both because women, especially older women, loved him. His general fecklessness about a more traditional career caused us some consternation, but then again, my grandfather had been a bartender. My uncle was a bartender. All right, they *owned* the bar, but it is also fair to say that our family had both its traditional careers—my father the hospital executive, my uncle the attorney, my mother the teacher and school director—and its less traditional ones—my cousins the chefs, another uncle a cook turned Major League Baseball clubhouse manager. I was a bit of a hybrid myself, at the time a low-level manager at a big nonprofit who was doing a very bad job of starting the creative-writing career that I'd gone to school for.

We'd tried to steer Nate toward something a little more stable. He'd made an abortive move to Los Angeles with a friend, thinking he would get a job in the restaurant industry, but everyone in LA was charming and good-looking and trying to get into the restaurant industry. Our dad got him into school to become an x-ray technician. He graduated and worked for a little while at a hospital before they busted him for coming to work high. He failed a drug test. He told me he'd been partying with friends the night before and he took something that wasn't what whoever had given it to him said it was. He told our parents something similar, edited slightly for what he imagined to be either their greater sensitivity or their greater naïveté about drugs. He went back to work at a bar.

The question of what, exactly, I might have done is one that I recognize intellectually as a question with a false premise. The past isn't a place you can return to. There is no *going back* armed with present knowledge that would have been, in retrospect, prescient. For example, I didn't know that my brother was addicted to painkillers. Perhaps I should have known. Some of my best friends had struggled frequently and fairly openly with heroin. I knew what their eyes looked like when they got high. I knew what furtiveness and long trips to the bathroom and the sudden onset of a kind of whole-person abstraction meant. I didn't recognize those things in my brother.

I knew he liked to party, but I thought it was mostly coke, in part because I'd seen him do coke, like a lot of bartenders, as a late-night prop to some after-hours drinks. I thought it was a harmless vice. *I* had done lines as a late-night prop to some after-hours drinks. I had—I still have—a laissez-faire attitude toward drugs. But I remember when I took my brother to his stint in inpatient rehab, drove him to the Greenbriar Treatment Center in Washington County, he'd said to me, "You don't steal to pay for coke." He had been fired from his last restaurant job for skimming. This was his way of telling me what he'd really been up to.

After he died, I gave a eulogy at his funeral service. I'm not a journalist, but I still have the habit of skimming to find the quotation I am looking for. I had a vague recollection of reading somewhere that the twelfth-century Jewish sage Maimonides (often known by the Hebrew acronym for his name, RMBM, or "Rambam") had a brother who died in a sea crossing, and Wikipedia conveniently obliged me with exactly the passage I wanted:

> The greatest misfortune that has befallen me during my entire life—worse than anything else—was the demise of the saint, may his memory be blessed, who drowned in the Indian sea, carrying much money belonging to me, him, and to others, and left with me a little daughter and a widow. On the day I received that terrible news I fell ill and remained in bed for about a year, suffering from a sore boil, fever, and depression, and was almost given up. About eight years have passed, but I am still mourning and unable to accept consolation. And how should I console myself? He grew up

on my knees, he was my brother, [and] he was my student.

After the funeral, our family friend Brian asked me where I'd found the quotation. Brian and his wife Ginny and their two sons, Adam and David, who were—or had been—the same ages as my brother and I, were very close to the family. Ginny and Brian had driven straight down from their lake house in upstate New York, ten hours, when my mother had called them with the news. Brian had been in advertising, and he recognized a slick pull quote when he heard one. I laughed—it was one of the first times I can remember really laughing after Nate died—and told him I got it online, although I had, in fact, searched the University of Pittsburgh library catalog to verify that the volume cited in the Wiki article existed. Brian laughed too, and he said, "Never bullshit a bullshitter."

He didn't mean, and I never took him to mean, that there was something fraudulent or insincere in what I said, and I still think the quotation was right for the occasion. In fact, as an atheist with certain superstitions about luck and coincidence that stand in for the more traditionally supernatural, I consider the universe's neat delivery of the actual citation for a hazy memory a mark of good fortune, something a little like fate. I'm mindful of this in *The Year of Magical Thinking*, which is also widely praised for the breadth of its reference, not because I think Didion is anything less than well read, and not because I consider it a sign of ersatz style and insincerity, but rather the opposite: I think that in her grief and fraught remembering, chance and good luck saw fit to help her recall, if only vaguely, the books and poems and passages that were precisely what she'd need.

CHAPTER 8

QUINTANA

Speaking of questions, the question of what Dunne and Didion's daughter, Quintana Roo, is doing in *The Year of Magical Thinking*, is a tough one. Of course, Quintana isn't actually *doing* anything. She was a real person to be sure, but she is also a character in a book, and no matter how seemingly true to life, a book is an artifact. The shape of it and all its contents is artifice. In "Sentimental Journeys," Didion's long essay on the "Central Park jogger" case, which was collected in *After Henry*, she reflects on the artificiality of *any* narrative: "The imposition of a sentimental, or false, narrative on the disparate and often random experience that constitutes the life of a city or a country means, necessarily, that much of what happens in that city or country will be rendered merely illustrative, a series of set pieces, or performance opportunities."

The passage is interesting, because while it is talking about a different sort of narrative than the very personal story that Didion is constructing in *Magical Thinking*, it gets at the difficulty of constructing a book around the easily paired crises of Dunne's death and Quintana's illness without forcing them into a neat counterpoint or lazily significant schema. (It's also worth mentioning that, to the parents of the accused boys in the jogger case, this narrative *was* a very personal story.) Several pages earlier in "Sentimental Journeys," Didion criticizes, as part of the "insistent sentimentalization of experience," something that she calls, presciently, "a reliance on certain magical gestures." Well, of course, there is the obvious narrative, chronological reason Quintana is there: her illness, and Didion's "handling" of it, bridge the last year of Dunne's life and the first year of Didion's widowhood.

It's also hard not to read Quintana's death backward onto *The Year of Magical Thinking*; it occurred very shortly afterward, so shortly that Didion was forced, a bit cruelly, to talk about it during the publicity tour. It later resulted in a sort of companion volume, *Blue Nights*, whose reception was significantly more mixed: many of those reviews seem to me to contain a

bit of tetchy disappointment that she'd failed to immediately produce a second masterpiece. *Blue Nights* is
not a masterpiece, but neither is it a failure in the way
that was sometimes implied by its critics.

And yet, though it's a mistake to make Quintana's
actual death an anachronistic component of *The Year
of Magical Thinking*, there's no doubt that the *pros-
pect* of her dying after a long and terrible illness does
serve to subtly amplify Didion's own worry that she
had somehow missed the signs of John's impending
demise, that she had blinded herself to the prospective
consequences of his state of health. But there is at the
same time an important contrast, because whatever
John Dunne's preexisting heart problems, his death is
nevertheless sudden and instantaneous. One moment
they're talking about "scotch or World War I," the next
he's "slumped motionless. At first I thought he was
making a failed joke, an attempt to make the difficulty
of the day seem manageable."

Quintana did not die instantaneously. Quintana
was dying. She was, moreover, frequently unconscious,
in an induced coma—between life and death.

Unusual dependency (is that a way of saying "marriage"? "husband and wife"? "mother and daughter"?

"nuclear family"?) is not the only situation in which complicated or pathological grief can occur. Another, I read in the literature, is one in which the grieving process is interrupted by "circumstantial factors," say by "a delay in the funeral," or by "an illness or second death in the family."

The "circumstantial factors" surround the fact that Didion's daughter was dying, and this is something that gets elided in discussions of *The Year of Magical Thinking*, which tend to note—as, to be fair, does the above excerpt from the book—that Didion spent much of the year after Dunne died dealing with their own daughter's critical illness. This isn't incorrect, per se, but what the formulation misses is that Quintana's crisis came first, that what occurred was not that Dunne died and then Quintana fell ill, but rather that Quintana was direly sick and then Dunne, suddenly if not without some forewarning, died.

CHAPTER 9

CIRCUMLOCUTION

The log for that evening showed only two entries, fewer than usual, even for a time of year when most people in the building left for more clement venues:

NOTE: Paramedics arrived at 9:20 p.m. for Mr. Dunne. Mr. Dunne was taken to hospital at 10:05 p.m. NOTE: Lightbulb out on A-B passenger elevator.

The A-B elevator was our elevator, the elevator on which the paramedics came up at 9:20 p.m., the elevator on which they took John (and me) downstairs to the ambulance at 10:05 p.m., the elevator on which I returned alone to our apartment at a time not noted. I had not noticed a lightbulb being out on the elevator. Nor had I noticed that the paramedics were in the apartment for forty-five minutes. I had always described it a "fifteen or twenty minutes." If they were here that long does it mean that he was alive? I put this question to a doctor I knew. "Sometimes they'll

work that long," he said. It was a while before I real-
ized that this in no way addressed the question.
   —JOAN DIDION, *The Year of Magical Thinking*

One of the things you notice when someone close to you has died is how reluctant everyone around you suddenly becomes just to say it. Now, I'm not entirely unsentimental, and although I inherited from my family—in particular from my dad's side of the family—a tendency to keep my cards close to my chest emotionally speaking and a possibly related habit of fairly blunt speaking, I don't object to a kind of simple decorum, a basic politeness, a certain reticence where the dead are concerned. To become totally unsentimental and totally skeptical is to become cold. There's a place for feeling. But whether it is out of an overabundance of politeness and decorum or simply a fear that the bereaved will—what, immediately kill themselves? If we speak too clearly about the presence and finality of death, we tend to speak in circles about the subject of death—which is, after all, *the* universal human condition.

Doctors, though they are supposed to be the least sentimental, the least affected by the quotidian but terrifying universality of human mortality, are often the worst offenders in this regard. That is in part because of a professional appreciation for the fact that medicine is not, as Didion would note in *Blue Nights*, an "exact science." It's in part because professional pride, which most doctors have in very large quantities, prefers to hedge against the possibility of a false or slightly inaccurate pronouncement. It's in part because doctors presume, with equal parts arrogance and pity, that the non–medical professionals who make up most grieving friends and family will fall to the sentimental and unsophisticated side and must be protected from their own limited capacity to understand.

The scene repeats itself. Quintana, having seemingly recovered, flies back to California with her husband, Gerry. She collapses again, just off the airplane. A friend calls from Los Angeles, and they reach Gerry at UCLA.

> One of the surgeons had just come out to give him an update. The surgical team was now "fairly confident" that Quintana would "leave the table," although they could not predict in what condition.

I remember realizing that this was meant as an improved assessment: the previous report from the operating room had been that the team was "not at all sure she would leave the table."

I remember trying and failing to understand the phrase "leave the table." Did they mean alive? Had they said "alive" and Gerry could not say it? *Whatever happens*, I remember thinking, *she will without question "leave the table."*

It occurs again, shortly thereafter, when Didion is trying to find out whether or not Quintana's fall had caused her to bleed into her brain or if bleeding in her brain had begun for some other reason and in fact caused her to fall. One surgeon is "one hundred percent sure" the trauma caused it. She presses him:

"It was the trauma, there was a ruptured blood vessel, we saw it," I thought he said. This had not seemed to entirely address the question—a ruptured blood vessel did not categorically rule out the possibility that the ruptured blood vessel had preceded and caused the fall—but there in the Café Med courtyard with the small balding man spitting on my shoe I realized that the answer to the question made no difference. It had happened. It was the new fact on the ground.

Which gets to the obverse side of the tendency toward circumlocution, which is our desire for a false specificity as a bulwark against a more general and terrible truth.

Didion's interactions with doctors and medical professionals throughout *The Year of Magical Thinking* actually provide some of the levity in the book—one of the reasons it is not, per Robert Pinsky, "a downer." You have to imagine the various medical and support staffs found her slightly terrifying and utterly infuriating, this tiny, aging woman who is obviously somewhat famous and unable to stop asking questions, particularly after she has immersed herself in, or at very least widely skimmed, the relevant literature. She is frustrated by doctors, confused by them—elsewhere, she thinks most of the professional and academic literature on the psychology of grief little better than cant—but she is never overawed by them.

I admit to finding these bits particularly funny for largely personal reasons. My father was a hospital executive, and so I grew up thinking of the docs, as we called them, rather like a stable of star athletes:

overpaid, ingenious—preternaturally so—at several very particular things, frequently very stupid, egotistical, petulant, and in strong need of organizational direction. I've never entirely outgrown that sensibility, and so I find Didion's hectoring of them vaguely admirable and always amusing.

It's interesting to think of the role of doctors in the overall construction of *The Year of Magical Thinking*, and in turn in our shared narrative of death, because although there are rites and funerals, although there are actual priests, although there is a whole literature of illness, dying, and grieving, the real priestly role in a modern, relentlessly scientific society has in fact fallen to that stable of star athletes. More than anyone or anything else, the doctors stand at the doors of death.

I had done it. I had acknowledged that he was dead. I had done this in as public a way as I could conceive.

Yet my thinking on this point remained suspiciously fluid. At dinner in the late spring or early summer I happened to meet a prominent academic theologian. Someone at the table raised a question about faith. The theologian spoke of ritual itself being a form of faith. My reaction was unexpressed but negative, vehement, excessive even to me. Later I realized that my immediate thought had been: *But I did the ritual. I did it all. I did St. John the Divine, I did the chant in Latin, I did the Catholic priest and the Episcopal priest, I did* "For a thousand years in thy sight are but as yesterday when it is past," *and I did* "In paradisum deducant angeli."

And it still didn't bring him back.

The idea that John Gregory Dunne might come back is, of course, the most exact and literal "magical thinking" in the book of that name.

But this gets back to the question of circumlocution, and in fact to a problem inherent in speaking too precisely, too medically, too scientifically about death, which is this: the doctor can only tell you he died. The autopsy can only tell you how he died. Neither of them can tell you that he passed away and is *gone*.

CHAPTER 10

FAMILY HISTORY

In a piece that appeared in *Vanity Fair*, entitled, in the weird instruction-manual prose that publications have adopted for the online era, "How Joan Didion the Writer Became Joan Didion the Legend," Lili Anolik ("Can Hollywood Handle Decent, Modest, Good-Humored Chris Hemsworth?" "Sofía Vergara, Hollywood's Hysterical, Business-Savvy, Unapologetic Sex Symbol") opens by offering that we—not Anolik, perhaps, but the rest of us—have got Joan Didion "wrong":

> And not just wrong, egregiously wrong, wrong to the point of blasphemy. I'm talking about the canonization of Didion, Didion as St. Joan, Didion as Our Mother of Sorrows. Didion is not, let me repeat, not a holy figure, nor is she a maternal one. She's cool-eyed and cold-blooded,

and that coolness and coldness—chilling, of course, but also bracing—is the source of her fascination as much as her artistry is; the source of her glamour too, and her seductiveness, because she *is* seductive, deeply. What she is is a femme fatale, and irresistible. She's our kiss of death, yet we open our mouths, kiss back.

This is all slightly overheated and embarrassing, and the article goes on to compare Didion to Warhol (because one cannot write about a significant figure from the sixties and not compare her to Warhol), and to back-project a vaguely Freudian reading of Didion's fiction onto her marriage with Dunne. And there's also something a bit silly about imagining a woman who fronted for a Céline campaign in her eighties as a holy figure; whatever else Didion may be associated with in her later life and career, she is still a famous clotheshorse.

There is, however, a kernel of truth in the worry, although I would hardly say that the problem is canonization for the wrong reasons. The degree to which Didion is now associated with the last couple of books she has produced, and that she is therefore taken as the sort of foremost expert on how terrible it is when spouses and children die, is unfortunate. It misses something fundamental about her methods and interests. "Something about a situation will bother me, so I will write a piece to find out what it is that bothers me," she said. It strikes me that, over her last three books, actually, beginning with *Where I Was From,* she has written not just an autobiography, but a family history.

A joke among some writer and editor friends of mine is that in order to win a major award, a novel's flap copy must include the words "sprawling" and "multi-generational." It's facetious, but it's not wrong. There's an enduring belief among the gatekeepers of American literature that realism of a nineteenth-century sort still represents the highest possibility of literary achievement. It occurs to me that, taken together, there's a bit of nineteenth-century realism in the triptych of *Where I Was From, The Year of Magical Thinking,* and *Blue Nights.* There's something Russian about it, the way it starts with genealogy and ends in funerals. I have been thinking about family history and genealogy lately, because I'm in my middle thirties and my grandparents are on their way out. Fritz, of course, my paternal grandfather, died years ago, but he was my oldest grandparent and was already in his mid-eighties. His widow, my grandmother Lena, is a healthy outlier at a disconcertingly spry ninety-two. But my maternal grandparents, Myrna and Mel, Gramme and Pappa, are dying.

The first thing to know about them is that they've been divorced for fifty years. Myrna remarried and divorced again. She was born in the Bronx, and when she was a young woman, she got a job in an advertising firm in Manhattan, a firm which made an appearance in *Mad Men*, thrilling her to no end. She met my grandfather after the war and married him for reasons that remained largely mysterious to her, although as she got older, especially after her stroke, her good-natured incredulity at having gone through with it in the first place changed into something more like a mission of salvation. "I thought I could change him," she told me over dinner one night last year—from what, or into what, I'm not quite sure.

"We were from New York. Everybody yelled," she said. "But your grandfather's family, they were *Southern*." This is true in a literal sense. Melvin Kobre came from a family of fairly genteel Southern Jews—a type that people forget exists, although in fact the first major population of Jews in North America was Southern, a community based in Charleston, South Carolina. Mel was from a little town called Danville, located at almost the exact midpoint of the southern border of Virginia, about fifty miles north of Greensboro, North Carolina. These were facts that I knew, as I knew that Mel had sold shoes before going to work for his more prosperous brother-in-law, who had a furniture company in High Point. (Or was that my great-grandfather, Myrna's dad? I have asked again since, and there seems to be some disputation on the point.) I knew that this work had taken him on the road; he'd been a traveling salesman for the rest of his working life. He was still working when my brother and I were boys, before his eyesight got too bad and he was forced to retire. I can still remember the giant Cadillac that he drove, which—though I was too young to notice at the time—was very out of place in the bland and middle-class but not quite prosperous condo development where he lived until he moved back south to a retirement home. He and Myrna, even after the divorce, had both lived in Columbus, Ohio. I knew in a vague way that this had been the center of his territory, that he and my grandmother had moved there shortly after my mother was born.

In fact, my grandmother had never really mentioned my grandfather's Southernness before her stroke. The idea that it had any significant impact on the development of his character wasn't something that came up. My grandfather's fastidious saving, his penchant for never having fun even though he had the means to do so, his general aversion to new experiences—these were topics of conversation, and Myrna would note them as a contrast to her own life, which, though precariously leveraged for most of her postdivorce years, was *fun*.

But after Myrna had a stroke, after my mom and dad convinced and cajoled her into deciding that she should move to Pittsburgh where the three of us lived, she began to emphasize Mel's Southern upbringing to explain certain aspects of his character, as she likewise began to talk more about her own childhood and youth in New York. I attribute both in part to the fact that the stroke affected her short-term memory. It became difficult for her to follow the thread of an extemporaneous conversation, but she was still able to tell stories, which developed into a kind of fixed repertoire. By "Southern," my grandmother meant that grandfather came from a family of extreme reticence: "They'd lean over to you and say, 'Now don't tell anyone, but….'" She implied a kind of Gothic secretiveness that was—if we're being honest—at least as much a derivation of the movies and plays she adored as it was of her former in-laws' actual lives.

Yet the essential fact to know about my grandfather, and the actual Gothic secret that I didn't learn myself until I was in college, was that his father, my great-grandfather, had killed himself when Mel was still a boy. "I was married to Mel for four years before he told me," Myrna says, and I see no reason to disbelieve her on this particular point. We were always under the impression that he'd hanged himself, that he'd had some business failures and some debts. Only very recently— my uncle Mike did some research and found some old copies of the Danville newspaper the *Bee*—did a more awful and more Tennessee Williams–worthy story emerge. My mom was unhappy that her brother had shared all this with Myrna, whose physical and mental health was still declining, but I'm fairly convinced that the revelations rather pleased my grandmother; they made her story better, more like a movie, and she told it to me almost every time I saw her thereafter. My great-grandfather hadn't been so much a failed businessman as a con man—he "dealt in bankrupt stocks," according to the *Bee*—whose confidence schemes were about to catch up to him. And he hadn't hanged himself; he'd poisoned himself to death with strychnine, as reported on page one of the *Bee* on December 15, 1933[*].

---

[*]In a sad and uncanny irony, in the months between the writing of this passage and the publication of this book, both grandparents died—Mel in November of 2016, and Myrna not quite a year later, in September of 2017.

CHAPTER 11

A PANAMA HAT AND A PAIR
OF OLD GREEK SHOES

Of the many indelible images and observations in *The Year of Magical Thinking*, the one mentioned most frequently is that of Joan Didion, unable to get rid of John Dunne's shoes because he might need them when he returns from the dead. I've always felt that this example of her magical thinking is meant to be taken both more and less literally than reviewers imagine, and I've never read it without thinking of the stories of ancient Egyptians, buried with all of their earthly possessions, which they would need in the afterlife, or the Greeks buried with a coin in their mouths in order to pay the boatman who ferried them across the river to the underworld. These stories, half archaeology and half myth, are generally treated in our popular culture as elements of basically primitive superstitions—even though our own funerary and burial rites are actually no more sensible, more profound, or less metaphysically questionable. In fact, a persistent myth in contemporary life is that the people in prior eras of history were hopeless literalists about their ritual and spiritual practices, that they literally believed the pharaoh would awake in the afterlife in need of his best crockery. By the same token, we might imagine a twenty-first-century deceased might find himself at the pearly gates, thankful that his still-living beloved stuffed him into a coffin in his best suit and with a nice layer of foundation. By the same token, we might imagine that John Gregory Dunne—returned from the dead or as a shade of himself—would literally need his shoes.

What interests me is the way in which the literal-metaphorical interpretations of this image are a doubled reflection of the mirror image of Didion the writer and Didion the grieving wife, Didion the portraitist and Didion the subject. There is, on one hand, the Didion who is "literally crazy" with grief, who refuses to throw out Dunne's suits or shoes because he may need them. But this Didion is also an artifact, a telling by a woman who is writing a book about her year of magical thinking. Because the period of time in which the book was written was in such close proximity to that year, because they effectively overlapped, because she "had made no changes to that file since I wrote the words, in January 2004, a day or two or three after the fact," it becomes very difficult to disentangle Joan Didion from Joan Didion, the literal from the metaphor, and the ritual from the belief.

The obvious reference here is Didion's own famous self-description from the introduction to *Slouching Towards Bethlehem*: "My only advantage as a reporter is that I am so physically small, so temperamentally unobtrusive, and so neurotically inarticulate that people tend to forget that my presence runs counter to their best interests. And it always does. That is one last thing to remember: *writers are always selling somebody out.*"

The last line gained a certain notoriety, since it suggested a kind of deliberate treachery or betrayal of confidence. Years later, in a long interview with Connie Doebele on C-SPAN in 2000, Didion explained what she had meant:

> I don't think anybody gains a great deal from having a reporter or a writer in their life. I think that…I wrote a line once that a lot of people have misinterpreted, in the introduction of *Slouching*

Towards Bethlehem, and the line was that writers are always selling someone out. Almost universally it was taken to mean that the writer is deliberately betraying…that's not what happens. What happens is the writer sees the subject in a different way from the way subject sees him or herself. People who are not public figures, people who have not dealt with public persona, generally don't have a very developed idea of how they transmit themselves, of how they look to other people.… No matter how sympathetic, no matter how positive the reporter's reaction may be, it is different from the way they view themselves.

The interview is worth watching in its entirety to get a sense of just how "physically small," "temperamentally unobtrusive," and "neurotically inarticulate" Joan Didion could be, although on reflection she is not so much inarticulate as hesitant. Like a lot of writers, she is more comfortable with a blank page than a physical silence to fill extemporaneously with words. I'm sure a much more academic book than this could be written—has been written—about the fine and subtle distinctions between presentation and representation, but I find her observation here especially compelling in retrospect. Didion was always at least in part her own subject but not necessarily intimately so. If it's unfair to say that she was only ever concerned with surfaces, then it's still fair to note that she was interested in gesture and didn't consider it superficial. Well, what is gesture but the first step toward ritual, and what is magical thinking but the gesture and ritual of a congregation of one? What's so noteworthy, in this context, is something Didion says much earlier in the interview, near the beginning. Doebele asks, "Do you do this very often? Sit down and talk about your writing?" and Didion says, "No, no I don't."

"No matter how sympathetic, no matter how positive the reporter's reaction may be, it is different from the way they view themselves."

CHAPTER 12

ADDICTION AS METAPHOR

I will not forget the instinctive wisdom of the friend who, every day for those first few weeks, brought me a quart container of scallion-and-ginger congee from Chinatown. Congee I could eat. Congee was all I could eat.

—Joan Didion, *The Year of Magical Thinking*

Something about Didion's description of her marriage and her description of its sudden end reminds me of the language we use to talk about addiction. That shouldn't be surprising. For me, *The Year of Magical Thinking* is all tied up with my memories of my brother's death from addiction. Or, it's more accurate to say, his death from a minor congenital heart defect that might not have been fatal, might never have been detected (or might have been fatal, might have been detected; there is no way to ever know, and to consider it too much is torture) had he not also been a habitual user of a variety of substances which can all have deleterious effects on the functioning of even an otherwise healthy heart.

And in fact it's fair to say that my whole life has been unusually afflicted by addictions, though not my own. I have no metric to measure "unusually" against. It only feels unusual to me, although I suspect that it's just a normal human condition to imagine ourselves as either uniquely blessed or uniquely cursed. My best friend—brother aside—has spent his whole life since adolescence careening between a sort of extremely hale wellness and periods of terrific, drug-fueled self-degradation. Other close friends of ours, several of whom are still very close and fortunately, miraculously alive, likewise spent years with needles in their arms. Other friends of theirs, people with whom I had—can I say fortunately? fortunate for whom?—more passing acquaintances, did die of overdoses or of the related common health afflictions of junkies.

My ex-boyfriend—we lived together for seven years altogether, though not uninterruptedly—was an alcoholic. Is an alcoholic? One of the central tenets, maybe the central tenet, of Alcoholics Anonymous and its related twelve-step sobriety programs is that addiction is at once a disease and a state of being. Like cancer, it can go into remission, but it can't ever be cured. One can be sober, as one can be cancer-free, but one never stops being an alcoholic. Let me, like Didion, quote from the opening pages of a book on the subject:

> I want to describe not what it's really like to emigrate to the kingdom of the ill and to live there, but the punitive or sentimental fantasies concocted about that situation; not real geography but stereotypes of national character. My subject is not physical illness itself but the uses of illness as a figure or metaphor. My point is that illness is *not* a metaphor, and that the most truthful way of regarding illness—and the healthiest way of being ill—is one most purified of, most resistant to, metaphoric thinking. Yet it is hardly possible to take up one's residence in the kingdom of the ill unprejudiced by the lurid metaphors with which it has been landscaped.

I don't suppose the irony of her own metaphors escaped Sontag when she wrote *Illness as Metaphor*. Emigrate to the kingdom of the ill and all. In any case, it's telling that the confused jargon that once surrounded cancer (and still does, though to a much lessened degree) continues to surround addiction. After all, we "battle" addiction. We blame it on failures of will and foibles of psychology. We don't mention it in the obituaries. "He was with us too briefly," I wrote in my brother's obit. I am, in fact, open when people ask how he died. "He struggled with addiction." Struggled. That is perhaps also a euphemism.

It isn't, however, *how* he died. It is, maybe, *why*, at least in a small, proximate sense. *How* he died is alone in a motel room in Uniontown, PA, full of pills that made his faulty heart stop working. He had been in rehab, then out of rehab. He'd shown signs of recovery whose glow couldn't dispel the fog of countering evidence. He remained cagey, haughty about his problems. He treated his therapist as he'd treated teachers in high school, when he was a mediocre student at best whose charmed instructors never failed to give him one letter grade better than he probably deserved. Regrettably it worked; his therapist was, like everyone who ever met him, infected, if I can use *that* metaphor, by his charms. He wouldn't go to group sessions beyond a few early, desultory, mandatory attendances. He knew that he wasn't like those people, those losers, the unemployed, pitiable half-people without lives or friends, nothing like him.

I'm not sure Nathan could have survived the realization that they were people *exactly* like him. (The conditional tone of that sentence is probably wrong. He did not, at last, survive it.) If we thought of him as a boy, then it was to our discredit; he wasn't. He was twenty-six years old. He was a man, although he was a man who no longer had a job or a fixed residence besides his parents' house or a girlfriend or any friends other than the drug friends who are the inevitable consequence of a shared affinity for the same high. It was inevitable, in retrospect, that he would go into a quick decline. It was inevitable that he would steal from my parents. It was inevitable that, having exhausted every other option, we would try—this is also AA or Al-Anon cant—to "separate with love." It was inevitable that when, after exhausting months of *dealing with him*, Mom and Dad and I would decide to take a vacation together to the Outer Banks, where we'd gone every summer when Nate and I were kids.

Didion writes, apropos Quintana's second extended hospital stay:

> One thing I noticed during the course of those weeks at UCLA was that many people I knew, whether from New York or in California or in other

places, shared a habit of mind usually credited to the very successful. They believed absolutely in their own management skills. They believed absolutely in the power of the telephone numbers they had at their fingertips, the right doctor, the major donor, the person who could facilitate a favor at State or Justice. The management skills of these people were in fact prodigious. The power of their telephone numbers was in fact unmatched. I had myself for most of my life shared the same core belief in my ability to control events....Yet I had always at some level apprehended, because I was born fearful, that some events in life would remain beyond my ability to control or manage them. Some events would just happen. This was one of those events. *You sit down to dinner and life as you know it ends.*

I recognize my family in this passage. We were maybe more local. I might substitute a DA or a chief of police for State and Justice. We did know a lot of doctors. We were a professional and well-to-do family. We knew attorneys, business owners, psychologists, politicians. Dad could drive to Harrisburg and get a meeting with the speaker, maybe even the governor.

It was probably inevitable that, around the time we got to the outskirts of DC, we got a call from my parents' neighbor, Dave. The alarm was going off at the house. Someone had tried to pry open one of the back windows. Who else could it have been but my brother, tired of crashing on the couches of not-really-friends, figuring he could slip in and lie low in the comfort of the four-bedroom colonial where he grew up? We drove back.

It was early summer, and I can remember sweating as Dave and my Dad and I put plywood over the window until a new one could be ordered and the contractor could come out to install it. It was zucchini season, and Bill showed us a grotesquely large one that had ballooned all out of ordinary proportion after a recent rain. I gardened too, back in Pittsburgh, and I said, "Man, yours is even bigger than mine." And Dave raised an eyebrow and said, "Well, I don't like to compare." The phrase is gallows humor, although they never tell you who is on the way to the gallows.

I was still talking to my brother intermittently. I asked him if it had been him. He denied it. He may have been living with a woman at the time, another pill and heroin user, but that soured, or else it passed in the way that friendships of shared convenience usually do. He hadn't worked in quite a while and was totally broke. He tried to forge my name and my dad's name on checks and to cash them at payday lenders—he actually succeeded a couple of times, and we managed it. We knew the right people. Then he was living in his car. Then, briefly, a rapprochement. Some contrition. A few phone calls. A few promises to change. And we thought, maybe this is rock bottom. That's also an AA term. My ex used it, and if I was skeptical of AA, it seemed to work for him, so maybe he had some insight, and maybe it would work for Nate.

My dad was as yet too skeptical and suspicious to let Nate move back into their house, but, as an intermediate step, arranged for him to stay at a little motel in town. It was July. It would be his birthday, and we made plans for a family dinner. I hadn't talked to him since the checks, but I talked to him then, and I had never heard him more excited about anything. The thing to understand is that we had been a very close family. We ate together all the time. There shouldn't have been anything special about it. There should have been no reason to be excited. Then Dad called me at work and told me he was gone. The people at the motel had suspected something was wrong. He'd driven over to the motel himself. They'd been unable to break open the door and had to wait for the police.

"Police are trying to figure out what happened to a man who was found dead in a motel room in Uniontown," WPXI, the local news station, reported. "Police said Nathan Bacharach, 26, was found dead at about noon on Thursday at the Heritage Inn.

"Police said Bacharach was locked inside the room. Police broke down the door of the room, where officers found him dead."

I've always wondered, but been too uncomfortable to ask anyone, even my own father, how it could have been that the people who ran the motel didn't have an extra key.

My recollections of what any of us did in the days immediately following are "mudgy," as Quintana called her memories of the days when she was most ill, the word Didon adopted to describe her memories of a large part of the year after Dunne died. But I can recall with real clarity the sensation—I have never experienced it before or since, of being acutely *not hungry* for days at a time. In *Blue Nights,* Didion recalls the day Quintana was born, which was the same day she and Dunne were able to adopt her:

After we left St. John's that night, we stopped in Beverly Hills to tell John's brother Nick and his wife, Lenny. Lenny offered to meet me at Saks in the morning to buy a layette. She was taking ice from a crystal bucket, making celebratory drinks. Making celebratory drinks was what we did in our family to mark any unusual, or for that matter any usual, occasion. In retrospect, we all drank more than we needed to drink but this did not occur to any of us in 1961. Only when I read my early fiction, in which someone was always downstairs making a drink and singing "Big Noise blew in from Winnetka," did I realize how much we all drank and how little thought we gave to it.

The Bacharachs enjoy their drinks as well, but mostly we were—not just Mom and Dad and I, but the grandparents and aunts and uncles and cousins—a family that ate. Someone was always putting out cheese and olives; Uncle Danny was always bringing peppers or stuffed mushrooms; Lena always had candy and cold cuts; Marty baked. After Fritz died, it felt like we all ate for days. I'd always been a skinny kid with a big appetite—even into adulthood, I ate like a teenager—and so the sensation not of being full but of being completely uninterested in food, of finding the idea of taking even one bite of anything almost repulsive, almost nauseous, stayed with me. Even when I was sick, I could eat. So I sympathize with Didion, who could only eat congee after her husband died. I know how she felt.

Interestingly, loss of appetite is also one of the acute symptoms of opiate withdrawal, both a stand-alone symptom as well as a consequence of the attendant symptom of extreme nausea. In fact, many of the physical and psychological conditions of withdrawal and grief are markedly similar: the physical dislocation, the weakness, the confusion, the paranoia and fear. Likewise, Didion's description of marriage bears a startling similarity to many depictions of addiction, whose synonym, after all, is *dependency*. I'll confess that I am deeply skeptical of much of the modern pathology and pseudopathology of drug and alcohol addiction, because it seems to me that there is something deeper and more universally human at work. Like a cancer represents not so much a disease like a cold or flu but a corruption of cells' own mechanisms for renewing themselves, so too does an addiction represent something ordinary and human grown out of control.

CHAPTER 13

A RIVER IN EGYPT

About a month after Didion published *Blue Nights*, *Jezebel*, the vaguely feminist sister site to the now-defunct *Gawker*, published an item called "Did Alcoholism Kill Joan Didion's Daughter?" As was often the case within the *Gawker* extended family, this turned out to be not so much an original piece as a gloss of another article on another website. The first article, written by Jennifer Matesa and entitled just a little less luridly "Is Joan Didion in Denial About Her Daughter's Alcoholism?" appeared in *The Fix*, a publication with a focus on addiction and recovery. In both instances, the writer speculates that Didion deliberately obscured Quintana's history of drug and alcohol use. Matesa writes, "While in *Magical Thinking* Didion inquires deeply and thoroughly into her husband's physical condition, in *Blue Nights*, Didion goes to some lengths to obscure from her readers, and perhaps even from herself, one fact in particular: it's likely that her daughter died of the consequences of alcoholism."

The piece goes on to diagnose remotely Quintana's real cause of death:

> Quintana died at 39 of acute pancreatitis. The U.S. National Library of Medicine reports that 70 percent of cases of acute pancreatitis in the U.S. are due to "alcoholism and alcohol abuse." In a 2009 article titled, "It's the Alcohol, Stupid," authors writing for a Nature Publishing Group journal state, "Overuse of alcohol is a major cause of acute and chronic pancreatitis in both developed and developing countries.…Prolonged overconsumption of alcohol for 5–10 years typically precedes the initial attack of acute alcoholic pancreatitis."

It's a compelling but circumstantial case. But even though I find it a believable (if unknowable) conclusion, I also find it slightly tawdry, because it's drafted into the service of a very particular insinuation, which is that Didion had in effect an affirmative moral obligation to write a different book, a book about her daughter, the alcoholic.

I recognize the implied moral duty from the years I spent living with a recovering alcoholic. Though the language of recovery insists on alcoholism and drug addiction as a "disease," sobriety, in the recovery community, also suggests a distinct moral element to one's addiction: it's a disease, yes, but also a condition heavily influenced by personal choice. This morality is heavily inflected by the cardinal sin of denial. Denial, after all, is the first and primary impediment to recovery, which can only begin when one admits that one has a problem. There is a deep philosophical contradiction here: the standard recovery liturgy is full of contradictory exhortations both to individual moral responsibility and to the fundamental necessity of admitting and accepting utter powerlessness as a precondition to any further improvement.

While criticizing Didion's failure or unwillingness to make a more explicit statement about the suspected cause of at least some of Quintana's health problems, Matesa makes another insinuation: "Yes, Quintana's father, John Gregory Dunne, did manage stress through alcohol. Right up to the very end of his life, in fact: on his final evening, after coming home from an extraordinarily stressful visit to the hospital where Quintana lay in critical condition, her father asked for a second scotch before he had finished his first, then, as he drank, he suffered a massive coronary event that killed him."

This is hastily tossed off, and it contradicts by implication an earlier assertion that Didion "inquires deeply and thoroughly into her husband's physical condition." I admit to having very little patience with this line of thinking in any case. The "power of denial," such as it is, is a part of the standard catechism of addiction in the United States, but it isn't empirical, and there is no evidence that the major systems and institutions of recovery in this country are in any meaningful way effective. Of course, the testimony of those for whom rehab or twelve-step recovery did work are often anecdotally powerful, but they are self-selective, and the sobering reality is that those seeking a sobriety synonymous with abstinence fail far more often than they succeed.

But I am still interested in this attitude toward *Blue Nights*, and by extension toward *The Year of Magical Thinking*, because I find that it echoes an earlier point of mine, central to my own understanding of these books, which is the degree to which we find ourselves, each individual reader, in an imagined conversation with what we read, the way the relationship feels less receptive than reciprocal. Part of the etiquette of reviewing literature is that a reviewer should try to avoid as much as possible the temptation to make a review into a suggestion about the book that the author *ought to have written*, to try to review the author's work *as it is*, good or bad, without implying that it should be altogether different from what it is. It's a fool's errand. In a way, it's the same illusion of neutral objectivity that Didion elsewhere criticized in political journalism, a clever professional fiction maintained for those who aren't quite in the know.

It's not fair to suggest that Didion ought to have written books that confronted more assiduously a very particular notion of personal denial and its power. It's also not fair to call the suggestion entirely unfair. Denial, of a sort, *is* the subject of *The Year of Magical Thinking,* as it is later the subject of *Blue Nights,* as it was the subject of *Where I Was From*. "Marriage is not only time: it is also, paradoxically, the denial of time." Denial is perhaps the central subject of Didion's oeuvre. Denial is the pathology from which springs the need to spin out, to "impose" a narrative line on the disparate and discontinuous events that constitute lived reality. I do not think, actually, that Didion was afraid to say that Quintana—or John, for that matter—was an alcoholic. I think, rather, that she distrusted the *story* of addiction, the American story of addiction, which must end in either personal triumph and life or personal failure and death. The stories we tell to make life bearable may simply be inadequate to the eradicating finality of death.

CHAPTER 14

LUCK

The question of luck is an uncomfortable one in America. The suggestion that good fortune might be unearned or bad fortune undeserved rubs against our central myth. If Didion is, as a writer, a great untangler and underminer of national myths, she is also, self-admittedly, a product of them. It's hard to escape the suspicion that the intensity of her grief results in part from a feeling that her luck had run out and in part from a resulting feeling that the bad luck was a kind of punishment for all the good that preceded it, a corrective to the unfair advantage of a lot of favorable breaks. It's one of the first things she says when Quintana wakes from her first induced coma and asks where her father is. "I told her what had happened," writes Didion. "I stressed the history of cardiac problems, the long run of luck that had finally caught up with us, the apparent suddenness but actual inevitability of the event."

I suppose "the apparent suddenness but actual inevitability of the event" is what interests me.

In my family, we were also very lucky. Far more than anything I've ever read, more than any course or film or teacher or individual experience, it was my family that established the way I think about the world. I can attribute a few vague attributes to the idea that I'm *an American*; I have certain affinities and a few affects of speech that mark me as a *Pittsburgher*; but I am concretely a Bacharach. We laugh the same way, we look the same, and we are, beyond the paper fact of our relations, something of a society of mutual aid. I can remember asking my mother—I might have been seven or eight—what would happen to Nate and me if she and Dad died. "That won't happen," she said, "but if it did, you'd go live with your John and Marty." Our aunt and uncle. Which seemed to me perfectly fine.

I do occasionally wonder, though, if the two years' difference between Nate and me had some minor but critical impact on the ultimate trajectories of our lives. We were well-to-do, increasingly so as we got older and our parents' careers—especially Dad's—advanced, and it goes without saying that to be well-off in America at the end of the twentieth and beginning of the twenty-first centuries is to be among the most materially fortunate of all the people who have ever lived in the history of the species. But I have some recollection of when we were poor. We weren't really poor; Dad was in graduate school, and Mom taught; their parents, my grandparents, helped them out, and we never wanted for anything necessary, but I have memories of the little rental houses, the carriage house on Card Lane, the duplex on Braddock, the weird white house on Harrison Avenue in Greensburg with sand instead of insulation in the walls. Nate might have remembered that last one. In any case, I ask myself sometimes if he had any innate sense that it was even possible to have anything other, or less, than everything we had.

Either way, the persistence of good luck rendered us unprepared for its opposite. How does a young man like Nathan die at twenty-six years old, a young man with "all the advantages," for whom the worst one can say of life is that it is an overwhelming menu of attractive and affordable choices? The truth is that even when things did go badly for him, when he broke his leg, when he dropped out of college, when he screwed up his move to California, when he messed up as an x-ray tech, the idea that there might be some ending other than it all working out remained largely unthinkable to us. It made us paradoxically both too harsh and too forgiving in our judgments of him: too harsh in that none of us could believe he could keep fucking up like that with so many people and so many resources at his disposal; too forgiving in that we allowed ourselves to believe, long after the counterevidence should have overwhelmed us, that he'd get it together, that it would all be perfectly fine.

"I kept saying to myself that I had been lucky all my life," Didion writes. My God, I recognize the feeling.

After I'd spoken to my father on the phone and he'd told me that Nate was "gone," I called my boyfriend and told him to get me at work. I stumbled into my boss's office and failed to precisely express why I was leaving immediately. My boyfriend picked me up—I remember he was with our friend Bryan—and drove me home. I think I packed an overnight bag, but I'm not sure. I don't remember. I drove down to Uniontown. We had moved there when I was in sixth grade. We'd lived for a little under a year in a terrible little bungalow near the fifth fairway of the Uniontown Country Club golf course while a house was built for us in a development called Heritage Hills. My father was the CEO of Uniontown Hospital. My mother was the director of a private two-year college called Laurel Business Institute. There were two routes: you could take the Turnpike to New Stanton and then go south on 119 until you hit the Uniontown bypass, or you could wind down Route 51 through the Monongahela Valley. I took 51. It had a lot of lights and a few speed traps, but it had no tolls, and I wasn't certain I could manage even that sort of simple transaction.

By the time I got to their house, to our house, the house where I'd lived since I was twelve years old, my Uncle Dan and Aunt Leslie were already there. My mother was pacing, then sitting, then pacing. They said that Ginny and Brian were on their way down from the lake. I remember nothing of the conversation, but at some point, Dad and Dan and I drove to the motel. The paramedics had taken Nate, but we had to collect his things.

You do not imagine, when you're boys growing up together, that you will one day go with your father and uncle to collect your brother's few remaining possessions from the motel room where he died. If you imagine it, you don't imagine he will have just turned twenty-six. You don't imagine that you'll go through his things first to find the drugs that may still be hidden somewhere so that your mother won't find them when she goes through them later on. You don't imagine going into the bathroom with your uncle, who lifts and checks under the lid of the tank on the toilet and makes a joke—not even a joke, just a comment—about his "misspent youth," nor that you'll almost laugh and be glad that he said it. You don't imagine that you'll find a few halved, unidentifiable pills in a ball cap in the underwear drawer and feel oddly disappointed that that was all, disappointed that there wasn't more evidence of *something*, disappointed that the scene isn't tragic and dramatic but tawdry and banal.

You didn't imagine it when he was still tending bar at the Elbow Room, when you used to go in almost every Thursday night, especially when you were fighting or broken up with your ex, and he would comp you a couple of glasses of Cab or Malbec, when you knew that he did coke, because you'd bummed a key bump or two yourself. He was twenty-four, twenty-five. You were what, twenty-seven? It all seemed so utterly harmless and ordinary.

Before he ever went to rehab, back when it seemed like he was just screwing up at work and screwing up in general, I had a conversation with my dad. "I know he's doing coke," Dad said. Nate had, on several occasions, taken weird calls and ducked out of a dinner or drinks. "I was alive in the eighties," Dad said. Which was funny at the time. And I remember saying that, yes, I knew he did, but to be honest I didn't think it was a big deal; I didn't think it was a *problem*. He was a twentysomething bartender, and he partied with his friends after shifts sometimes. So what? I remember just before he went into rehab, when I had convinced myself that it was cocaine that was the problem, that I felt like an unbelievable liar, like the embarrassed brother who'd been covering for him, *enabling* as the language of recovery would have it. I remember when Nate told me it wasn't coke. "You don't steal to pay for coke." In the strictest sense, this isn't true. People do steal for coke. But that wasn't what he meant. What he meant was: OxyContin and heroin. I remember, very briefly, feeling a kind of preposterous and condemnable relief. I *hadn't* been covering for him when I said *that* wasn't his problem. I'd been right; it had been the truth. One of the things you learn when your little brother dies as Nate did is that there is very little inherent value in "the truth."

There's a passage in *The Year of Magical Thinking*, just after Didion admits that she'd considered herself to have "been lucky all my life," where she writes:

Quintana mentioned what she seemed to consider the inequable distribution of bad news. In the ninth grade, she had come home from a retreat at Yosemite to learn that her uncle Stephen had committed suicide. In the eleventh grade she had been woken at Susan's at six-thirty in the morning to learn that Dominique had been murdered. "Most people I know at Westlake don't even know anyone who died," she said, "and just since I've been there I've had a murder and a suicide in my family."

"It all evens out in the end," John said, an answer that bewildered me (what did it mean, couldn't he do better than that?) but one that seemed to satisfy her.

Several years later, after Susan's mother and father died within a year or two of each other, Susan asked if I remembered John telling Quintana that it all evened out in the end. I said I remembered.

"He was right," Susan said. "It did."

I recall being shocked. It had never occurred to me that John meant that bad news will come to each of us. Either Susan or Quintana had surely misunderstood. I explained to Susan that John had meant something entirely different: he had meant that people who get bad news will eventually get their share of good news.

"That's not what I meant at all," John said.

"I knew what he meant," Susan said.

Had I understood nothing?

CHAPTER 15

THE DEAD STAR

I didn't stay at my parents' house that night. I drove back to Pittsburgh, because I'd said that I would drive to Columbus, Ohio, the next morning to pick up my maternal grandmother, Myrna, and bring her back to Pennsylvania for the funeral. At the time, I was driving a little purple Saturn, which I'd bought from the estate of my uncle's sister-in-law's not-quite-ex-husband after he'd died a few years earlier. That probably seems convoluted, but for a certain kind of family in a city like Pittsburgh, your uncle's sister-in-law's not-quite-ex-husband is a person with whom you retain a visceral connection. We decided that a little purple Saturn was probably not the best for my grandmother to sit in; she was nearly eighty at the time and had a bad back and bad knees, so I left it at my parents' and borrowed my mom's car, a big 2007 Lexus. Five years later, I'd give the Saturn to my cousin Joe, my uncle Dan's son, and my mom would give the Lexus to me. I still drive it. Yet it never occurred to me, not until I wrote this paragraph, that I've been driving, and will continue to drive for the foreseeable future, the car that I'd taken to pick up my grandmother and drive her to Pittsburgh for the occasion of the funeral of her younger grandson.

Now Myrna is dying, albeit slowly, and not without giving my mom a hell of a hard time about it. We're all dying, of course; it's our one inexorable, immutable end. But there's a threshold one crosses in which the ultimate destination becomes the trajectory of the current trip, when death is no longer a fixed point on the horizon of a desert highway but rather a rapidly approaching exit.

"Don't ever get old," she said to me, when Mom and Dad and I were visiting her in the rehabilitation center where she resided—where, I'm quite certain, she considered herself interned—temporarily after her second stroke in three years.

My father and I exchanged a glance. "Well," I said as lightly as I could, "there's not really anything anyone can do about that." But she'd stopped listening.

My grandmother was still living in Columbus when she had her first stroke. She'd been having some health problems—a bad heart and recent pacemaker implant, her always troublesome knees, very high blood pressure, symptoms that probably represented prediabetes—but was still living alone and managing it. We had broached the subject of her moving to Pittsburgh to be closer to all of us, to be closer to my dad's side of the family, to be able to come to the dinners and Christmases and seders of the whole raucous, blended group, but she resisted. She knew people in Columbus. She was *someone* in Columbus. This latter characterization was by then more notional than actual. She hadn't really worked in years. Her friends had died or moved away. Her social circle wasn't what it once was. She still played bridge and mah-jongg, but beyond that, she watched a lot of classic movies on TV and ate too much candy in her apartment. Alone.

In my adult life, I'd always found Myrna to be a vain but admirable woman. After she married my grandfather, after my mother was born, after my grandfather went to work selling furniture for his brother-in-law, they moved to Ohio, his new territory. They lived in Coshocton, a little town about halfway between Columbus and Canton with nothing to commend it but the fact that it was vaguely central and Myrna's sister lived there. But her sister and her sister's husband were among the town's Jewish petite bourgeoisie. They belonged to a social club. They had connections. They entertained. Whereas my grandparents were and had none of these things. They lived in an apartment complex. My grandfather was gone Monday to Friday every week. My uncle was born. Myrna couldn't drive, and the only people she knew lived in their complex, other wives, mostly, whose husbands were often away.

Myrna insisted that she learn to drive. They moved to Columbus. They needed money. A girlfriend suggested she try selling real estate. She made a deal. She made a few more deals. She willed herself into a career as an agent despite my grandfather's inarticulate discomfort idea at the idea of her working as she did. "And I never went to college," she'd tell me. My mother and then my uncle went away to college. She and Mel divorced. She kept working. She ran her own office for a big Columbus firm. She became the first woman president of the Ohio Real Estate Association. She remarried a developer named Neil. "He had business with my office, but he insisted on talking to me and not to one of my agents. Then he asked me to have dinner. He was ten years younger than me!"

They married. He had a plan for a condo development. She insisted on being part of the deal, investing her own money. She didn't have very much to invest. Myrna, as she'd later confess to me, always preferred to be the boss, the president, to the drudgery of office business. She liked the appearance of success. She had always styled herself after the tough women heroines of the movies she loved, right down to a Hepburn affect to her speech. This preference for superficies over labor left her well regarded but undercapitalized. Yet she got her wish: she got her portion of the partnership. They built the condos, a modern development of sprawling mod townhouses on Big Walnut Creek on the southeastern side of Columbus. She and Neil lived in one of the higher-end units themselves. The properties didn't move. The location was wrong. The bottom fell out of the market. They lost their shirts. She and Neil divorced. She moved into the Summit Chase, a high-rise in Grandview, where she'd live for the next twenty years, selling units and living in a white luxury condo with a view of downtown, ever in the red on her bottom line.

Her first stroke affected her vision and short-term memory; her second affected her speech and cognition more profoundly. It is the worst thing that could have happened to her, worse even than losing her second grandchild, my brother, because it is the thing she most feared, the future whose possibility she most strongly denied, continues even to deny. Because she long refused physical therapy and exercise, her knees have gone to the point where she can no longer really walk, not even with a walker. She is cogent, and she can still converse, but it exhausts her. She was a woman who lived in terror of getting old—or, who lived in terror of losing the ability to put on the appearance of not being old. She was afraid of finding herself a diminished presence within an uncooperative body, and that is exactly what she's become. "It would have been better if I'd just died," she said to my mother. It is a terrible thing to say to one's child.

I find myself thinking that it's a more unforgivable thing to say to a woman who's lost her son, because, as it happens—inevitably, inexorably—my grandmother's swift regression to a kind of second childhood (a petulant and histrionic childhood at that) places my mother in a position once again of having a person who, while technically an adult, is in every real respect my mother's dependent: another sick child, denying she has a problem and circling the drain. And yet my brother, I have to believe, at least *wanted* to live. He shared many traits with his grandmother, actually. He enjoyed luxuries that he couldn't afford. He was good at making money—he could hustle like no one's business—and lousy at keeping it. He'd spend a thousand dollars on a dinner when he had a hundred. He liked fast cars and fancy apartments. He had Myrna's irrepressible sweet tooth. But I am not able to process the irony of that boy who was my brother looking back across the plane that separates the living from the dead and seeing his grandmother, who is still living, perhaps against her better judgment. The irony of the specter (and I use that word advisedly) of a young man who should still be alive watching, across the abyss, an old woman who has begun to speak fondly of death.

There are a pair of passages fairly late in *The Year of Magical Thinking* in which Didion, having tried to go to Boston to cover the Democratic National Convention, breaks down almost immediately upon arrival. In the first, she writes:

> A week or so before the Democratic convention, Dennis Overbye of the *New York Times* had reported a story involving Stephen Hawking. At a conference in Dublin, according to the *Times*, Dr. Hawking said that he had been wrong thirty years before when he asserted that information

swallowed by a black hole could never be retrieved from it. This change of mind was "of great consequence to science," according to the *Times*, "because if Dr. Hawking had been right, it would have violated a basic tenet of modern physics: that it is always possible to reverse time, run the proverbial film backward and reconstruct what happened in, say, the collision of two cars, or the collapse of a dead star into a black hole."

Several pages later, after reflecting on a number of actual and missed opportunities with John, after thinking over his late-life insistence on "doing things not because we were expected to do them or had always done them or should do them but because we wanted to do them," she returns to the image:

I realized that since the last morning of 2003, the morning after he died, I had been trying to reverse time, run the film backward.

It was now eight months later, August 30, 2004, and I still was.

The difference was that all through those eight months I had been trying to substitute an alternate reel. Now I was trying only to reconstruct the collision, the collapse of the dead star.

My formal interest as a writer is the way that an image is planted almost as an aside only to be resurrected (can I use that word?) shortly afterward in a surprising and illuminating way. It's something that Didion does frequently and deftly, especially in *The Year of Magical Thinking*, often placing a suggestion at the beginning of a chapter or a subsection of a chapter that will return at an odd angle to surprise you later on.

Lately, though, I find myself thinking of the image of the black hole, of the intermittent yet possible escape of information from it, when I think about Myrna, whose mind likewise has begun to resemble a star in some state of collapse: still broadcasting, but weakly, radiating mostly back on itself. It also occurs to me that Didion is in a way exactly the woman my grandmother imagined herself to be, that the recent image of Joan Didion posing in dark glasses for a Céline ad is the self-image that Myrna still has of herself: older, yes, but still slim, in a big sweater and expensive dark glasses. A woman who'd known people in Hollywood, who went to the best restaurants, who traveled between New York and LA, who spoke with the clipped, bitten pronunciation of educated women of a certain era.

Myrna did love to read—her preferences ran to mysteries and thrillers; she bought biographies, but only to display on the coffee table—but could never write. She once told me that she wanted to write a novel based on the life and characters of the Summit Chase. She told me only last year that once she had "gotten settled, gotten everything taken care of" in Pittsburgh, she was finally going to write a history of her family, a narrative genealogy. She didn't get everything settled, everything taken care of, and she didn't write the history, and she would not now be able to. It strikes me, though, that I began to write this book not only out of admiration for another writer, not just because I was between novels and it seemed like an interesting project, but also because I am starting to realize how actually likely it is, through bad luck or bad choices or both, that we can, each of us ourselves, be the thing that collapses.

CHAPTER 16

MISFORTUNE

"Maimonides," I said at my brother's funeral, "called his brother's death 'the greatest misfortune that has befallen me during my entire life.' Of course," I went on, "he also called his brother a saint, and I don't suppose I'd be able to put that one past all of you, who knew him so well. He was a good kid who was struggling to become a good man, and whatever his faults, he loved his family without pause or condition, and although none of us knows or can claim to know what there is beyond the veil of death, I know that that love did not die and will never pass out of the world."

I am not, in retrospect, entirely sure I meant by that last part. Did I really know so much? How could I?

Nathan did not, in fact, love us without pause or condition. When his will was thwarted, he was capable of hating us, too. I remember, in the last two years of his life, how frequently he went back to the whet-stone with one particular dull blade. Our grandfather, Mel—who was already secured away for a decade-long decline in a North Carolina retirement home, who unlike his ex, Myrna, had never spent one red cent on anything like a luxury or pleasure for himself (you can imagine why they divorced)—had at some point given Nate and me gifts of ten thousand dollars each. Dad had socked that money away for us in some boring, fund-indexed vehicle, secure for some future first real-estate purchase or something. And, in fact, I did use mine, along with some invested bar mitzvah money, some mature State of Israel bonds (these also from Mel), and a couple thousand bucks from Mom and Dad, to make the down payment on a little row house near the river in the Lawrenceville neighbor-hood of Pittsburgh.

This fact—that my parents had *given me my money*—absolutely infuriated my brother. He wanted his ten grand, and he nursed a dark resentment toward all of us as if we were involved in a conspiracy against him. Actually, as I recall, Dad had given him access to a portion of his money years earlier; Nate had wanted to invest it himself. He had, as he always did, done very well, very quickly, and then blown his windfall on some dumb, frivolous shit. Dad's position in this case was straightforward and unbending. You can have your money just like Jake, but just like him, it's got to be *for* something. That my brother could not, by then, figure out some believable scam—some shell auto purchase or apartment project or vacation or anything other than angry demands for cash—indicates just how far gone he was into an addict's self-delusion. Ironically, I don't think any of us had the slightest notion of him as an addict when he first began asking for the loot. Later, though, when we knew, he kept asking.

I always thought he was angrier at me than he was at my parents, even though I was mostly a passive observer to his battle of wills with our father, a battle I doubt he'd have won if he were sober, let alone in the late stages of his affliction. They were an impediment to his desires, but I was the unjust recipient of their unfair distribution. I can remember driving with him, on our way to grab a drink or have dinner or see some action move—he was partial to the *Fast and Furious* franchise—when, unbidden, he'd start haranguing me about it, as if I'd cast some spell to disinherit him: "It's fucking bullshit! They gave you *your* money!"

I would try to make a joke of this: really, they'd given it to Coldwell Banker and to Citibank and to the old lady from whom I'd bought the house. It mollified him, but it never satisfied him.

I know he loved me. We'd bickered as children, but by the time we were in high school, we'd developed an uncomplicated friendship. Later, we hung out when I was home from college; I visited him in Morgantown when he was in college. We talked on the phone. When we lived in Pittsburgh, I saw him more than anyone other than my roommate or, later, my boyfriend. I even convinced him to move to Lawrenceville, even though he found its hipsters vaguely contemptible. We used to cook dinner together in the apartment he shared with his girlfriend. When I broke up with my boyfriend, who was an artist, Nate told me to come over and drink a bottle of expensive California Zin he'd bought (he was, in everything, a spendthrift). Really, he just wanted me to watch as he ceremoniously (and, I admit, cathartically) yanked one of my now-ex's huge paintings, a gift, off the wall of his living room.

But he also hated me. He thought our parents favored me. He thought the apparent stability of my life was a kind of intolerable smugness. If by lifestyle and association I was always the less traditional of the two, the queer one working in the arts and living in a neighborhood of the too-pierced and overtattooed, I was also the one with the normie job, a manager with business cards, a guy who owned a house with his boyfriend and threw overwrought dinner parties for his fancy friends. If I stayed out too late, I still went to the office the next day, even if I hid from my coworkers and let the phone ring to voicemail. I was—I remain—a little bit of a square.

Nate—who'd joined a frat, who'd never dressed in anything other than the style of a slightly gauche men's style magazine, who liked Miami Beach and some vague idea of Las Vegas, who snowboarded, for God's sake—was not. His capacity to party, for drugs and drink—but drugs especially—was super-human. "There he goes," Hunter S. Thompson said of his friend and attorney in *Fear and Loathing in Las Vegas*. "One of God's own prototypes. A high-powered mutant of some kind never even considered for mass production. Too weird to live, and too rare to die." I remember in my younger and somewhat druggier days thinking vainly that this applied to me, even though I was always—I remain—a lightweight. Nate was the weird one, and the rare one. But Nate died.

CHAPTER 17

RESISTANCE

When Quintana is in the hospital, after John has already died, there is a question of whether or not to give her a tracheotomy to assist her breathing, as opposed to continuing intubation through the mouth. Didion finds herself reluctant to agree to the procedure, even though it is observably the standard procedure in the neurological unit. The doctors reassure her:

> A trach could be done with fentanyl and muscle relaxant, she would be under anesthesia no more than an hour. A trach would leave no cosmetic effect to speak of, "only a little dimple scar," "as time goes by maybe no scar at all."
>
> They kept mentioning this last point as if the basis for my resistance to the trach was the scar. They were doctors, however freshly minted. I was

not. Ergo, any concerns I had must be cosmetic, frivolous.

In fact I had no idea why I so resisted the trach.

I think now that my resistance came from the same fund of superstition from which I had been drawing since John died. If she did not have a trach she could be fine in the morning, ready to eat, talk, go home. If she did not have a trach we could be on a plane by the weekend. Even if they did not want her to fly, I could take her with me to the Beverly Wilshire, we could have our nails done, sit by the pool. If they still did not want her to fly we could drive out to Malibu, spend a few restorative days with Jean Moore,

If she did not have a trach.

This was demented, but so was I.

My grandfather, Mel, Myrna's ex-husband, always had a tendency toward hypochondria, and although none of the poor workers at his nursing home deserved his equally advancing grumpiness, he took to actual advanced age with a kind of alacrity, as if it fulfilled a lifetime of *feeling* that he was old. Myrna, on the other hand, cannot abide the thought of it. My grandfather would, until dementia necessitated full-time care, call the ambulance at the slightest twinge of pain, demand prescriptions he didn't need, delight in telling me, for instance, how frequently this or that heart medicine made him have to pee. Myrna hates the idea of doctors, resists the simplest therapies, refuses the slightest necessary aid until the moment of inescapable and uttermost need. Regarding her own health, she exists in a state of denial that is impressive in a perverse way. She believes, if belief is the right word, that it will all, at some point, of its own accord, simply get better. Her vision will get better. Her knees will improve. Her strokes will not have happened. Her blood pressure will come down. But if she *admits* to any of these underlying weaknesses by seeking the right treatment, by going to physical therapy, by learning to properly use a cane or a walker or a wheelchair, then she will have removed the magical possibility that none of them are real. She will have admitted the possibility that she may wake up and it will *not* be fine.

It's very easy to complain that all this is utterly irrational, the behavior of a stubborn and vain woman who is ironically denying herself practical independence by refusing to deal with physical reality, yet I recognize so intimately this form of thinking, which attends so many traumas, large and small, in all of our lives.

I remember, for example, trying to explain once why I had stayed with T., my ex, for so long, long after the petals had fallen from the bud, after we'd broken up and gotten back together, after he'd had affairs, after I'd stopped caring whether he was or was not having an affair. Why did I stay with him, in fact, until he was the one finally to say that we should probably call it quits? I explained it as force of habit, as a comfortable and companionable lifestyle, as the inertia of having a house together and a dog and the same friends. There's truth in all of that. But the deeper truth is that, for a long time, I simply did not believe that it was bad, even though I knew it was so. If I were to admit what I knew, if I accepted it, then it would be real; I would admit to the possibility that I might wake up and it would *not* all be just fine.

We'd gotten back together after the last breakup because he got sober. That's obviously a flattening and a distortion of something complex and multidimensional. It's like a Mercator projection map: the right shape, but the wrong size at the poles. Nevertheless, it's the best picture I can draw, the best explanation of why it happened, and I am sure it's also the explanation I gave to my slightly befuddled family. "He's not drinking anymore," I told my mother, who is my mother, so of course: *as long as it made me happy*. Nate was much more unstinting. "That's stupid," he told me when I told him. "He's sober? *So what?*" This could not have been very long before Nathan's own problems with drugs became acute and obvious to us, so perhaps there was an element of self-defensive presentiment in it. Years later, after Nate had died, when T. and I broke up for good, I thought about it again. Right for the wrong reasons.

We broke up in June, just after I'd been hit by a car while riding my bike. The one had nothing to do with the other, but the proximity of the two events continues to make them seem to me suspiciously linked, the way the disparate evils of a conspiracy theory appear to the conspiracy theorist as inextricable pieces of the same plot. I'd been out on a long solo ride around the North Hills and East End of Pittsburgh. I'd swung through downtown, where an arts festival run by the company I worked for was underway. I was riding home—it was around 7:00 p.m.—on Smallman Street, a busy daytime thoroughfare in Pittsburgh's Strip District that empties out at the end of the workday until the bars and clubs open much later in the evening. I was, as cyclists say, hammering: riding faster and with more effort than the usual leisurely spin. It isn't actually accurate to say that I was hit by a car. Rather, a driver approaching from the opposite direction swerved left across my path, far too close for me even to apply the brakes. I threw the bike sideways as much as I could and smashed into the front passenger side of his hood. My chin put a pretty good dent in his A-pillar. My right knee, the first part of me to strike the car, popped. I would later learn that in addition to the stitches in my chin and the garden of bruises and abrasions all over my body, I had torn my right posterior cruciate ligament halfway through.

The emergency department of the hospital x-rayed me and CT scanned my head to make sure I hadn't suffered any kind of concussive trauma. But they didn't do any soft-tissue imaging of the rest of my body. I left the hospital very late that night thinking that the stiffness and immobility in my right leg, like the stiffness and immobility in the rest of my body, was general and would pass. It was only four or five days later, when the rest of me was feeling better but the right knee had gotten, if anything, even worse, that I panicked and hauled myself into the family health clinic around the block from me, where a young resident quickly diagnosed that something was wrong in the knee.

A few days later, calling in a few of Dad's connections, I was at the UPMC Sports Medicine clinic, where a self-involved but clearly expert sixtysomething orthopedic surgeon and his team diagnosed the exact nature of the injury. They told me that they could either try surgery or I could just do physical therapy, because "the truth is that half a PCL is about as good as the PCL from a cadaver that we'd use in surgery, and you'd still have to do physical therapy." I asked if I would be able to ride a bike like I had before. "You will definitely be able to ride a bike," he told me. You can see why I sympathize with Didion's complaint that doctors don't necessarily answer the questions that they're asked.

I did make a full, or nearly full, recovery, after seven months of thrice-weekly therapy and many more months of very easy riding. But in the couple of weeks after the accident, before I'd begun therapy in earnest, when I had to sit in the reserved-for-elderly seats on the bus in the morning because I couldn't bend my knee enough to sit in the regular ones, when I walked with a pronounced limp, it seemed entirely possible that I would never really ride a bike again, nor play tennis, nor go for a run or a hike in the mountains. That was when T. told me in the kitchen of the house that I'd bought at least in part because he'd liked it so much that it wasn't going to work between us. And, shortly thereafter, left.

He wasn't wrong, and I'd known it for years, yet it seemed the culmination of five years of terrible luck, the "collapse" as Didion called it, the "collision." I got back into a bad relationship, my brother died, I got hit by a car, my boyfriend left me. In each instance and collectively, I had ignored the clear signs and failed to take the appropriately ameliorative minor actions. I'd believed none of it could ever happen to me; when it happened to me, I couldn't believe that it had happened to me.

But I'm not convinced this is a pathology, a psychological malady. I am increasingly suspicious of the habit of dividing the world into the broad categories of those things which are good for us and those that are bad. Didion says:

> Only after I read the autopsy report did I stop
> trying to reconstruct the collision, the collapse
> of the dead star. The collapse had been there all
> along, invisible, unsuspected.

[…]

That was the scenario. The LAD got fixed in 1987 and it stayed fixed until everybody forgot about it and then it got unfixed. *We call it the widowmaker, pal*, the cardiologist had said in 1987.

I tell you that I shall not live two days, Gawain said.

When something happens to me, John had said.

1987. He died in 2004. How would she have lived without a little bit of denial, without *forgetting*, without believing that it could not, that it would not, happen to her? I'm not convinced it's possible to live when people die, when love fails and leaves us, when we are hit by swerving cars, without ignoring the internal actuary and believing, against all evidence of experience, that the "unthinkable" will *not* occur: the plane will not fall from the clear blue sky, the routine errand will not end on the shoulder with the car in flames, the children will play on the swings but the rattlesnakes will not strike from the ivy.

CHAPTER 18

THE QUESTION OF SELF-PITY

Earlier I wrote that I wasn't sure the question of self-pity was exactly the question that Didion was asking, which may seem like an interpretive leap, since Didion says that they were among "the first words I wrote after it happened." But I think her book bears out this interpretation. It just took a little while to figure out *why* I think so. There it is, in chapter six. After having described a sensation or vision of "what I believed at the time to be an apprehension of death" ("It was an effect of light"), and just before introducing again the question of self-pity, she writes this: "Why, if those were images of death, did I remain so unable to accept the fact that he had died? Was it because I was failing to understand it as something that had happened to him? Was it because I was still understanding it as something that had happened to me?"

I cannot tell you how deeply I still feel this way about Nathan. It isn't quite self-pity. It isn't woe-is-me. It's something else.

"This is the worst thing that ever happened to this family," my great-aunt Rosemarie said at his funeral. Could that really be the case? Worse than ancestral poverty in Calabria? Worse than the death of two of their siblings in childhood, one run down in the street in front of their house? Worse than their mother, my great-grandmother's illness and depression, so bad that my grandmother Lena all but raised Rosemarie by herself? Worse than any of the ordinary deaths from old age and illness or the hundreds of other little tragedies that strike every family?

I don't know, but you notice the same formulation: "that ever happened *to this family*." That happened to *me*. Yet strictly speaking, it *happened*, specifically, to *him*.

There's a poem by Galway Kinnell, "Freedom, New Hampshire," that begins in an almost Romantic manner, a series of picaresque wanderings with an unidentified companion through the rural territory of the poet's youth, only to slowly transform over its four distinct sections into something mystical and elegiac. It ends, rather than beginning, with a dedication:

"*For my brother, 1925–1957.*" I taught the poem in a workshop at Oberlin because I liked the way each section turns at a surprising angle to the last, because it treats in a contemporary way the classic material of something like Wordsworth's "Ode: Intimations of Immortality from Recollections of Early Childhood," and because I thought it was valuable to show novice poets (imagine: I was twenty-one and believed myself to be something other than a novice poet myself) how something so small as the decision to place a dedication at the end of the work had such a dramatic and total effect on the experience of reading it.

I always found the final stanza of the poem, just before the dedication, to be its loveliest, but it only occurred to me as I was writing this book how uncannily it speaks to exactly this question of him-or-me.

> But an incarnation is in particular flesh
> And the dust that is swirled into a shape
> And crumbles and is swirled again had but
>   one shape
> That was this man. When he is dead the grass
> Heals what he suffered, but he remains dead,
> And the few who loved him know this until
>   they die.

"It is true," Kinnell writes in the stanza prior, "[t]hat only flesh dies and spirit flowers without stop." "But" — that's a conjunction whose power is underappreciated, isn't it?— "…the dust…had but one shape / That was this man."

In whatever form we may personally believe a person persists—in love, in our memories, literally in spirit— the incarnation does end, irrevocably and absolutely. The question of self-pity, I think, is really one of persistence, of duration. It's a tiny difference with giant significance, the dedication delayed to the end of the poem that makes it a wholly different poem. Death is what happened to John Gregory Dunne. Death is what happened to Nathan Andrew Bacharach. Their *being dead* is what is happening to us.

CHAPTER 19

AN ORDINARY DAY

When I first started discussing this project with my editor, he sent along a sort of template describing how this and other books in this series might be structured. The template itself had a pretty indelible image in it: "Describe the hole in the universe that was shaped like our book." What he meant was: try to recreate the moment of the book's arrival, using the benefit of hindsight to show how obviously necessary that arrival was. (I like this idea, by the way. Ironically and unintentionally, one of the central themes of Wordsworth's ode is that the soul preexists the body, and maybe it's fair to say that a book, or at least the need for a book, preexists its actual writing.) And there's the nature of this book, *The Year of Magical Thinking*, and the less literal but still true notion that the "hole in the universe that was shaped like our book" was very much in the particular shape of John Gregory Dunne. And there's Kinnell again: "the dust that is swirled into a shape / And crumbles and is swirled again had but one shape / That was this man."

Also, though, there *is* the literal question, the real 2005 into which *The Year of Magical Thinking* was born. I admit to having a hard time with this one. What does one say? That it was at the weird inflection point of the Bush era? That Hurricane Katrina *happened*? That Muqtada al-Sadr was rising in Baghdad? That there was a royal wedding in England? That Cardinal Ratzinger began his brief tenure as Pope Benedict XVI? That a few people were beginning to get a sense that there was something really, fundamentally wrong in the markets and in the financial sector, which would a couple of years later blow up spectacularly? None of these things seems precisely right.

Then, just recently, I came across, of all things, an *LA Review of Books* essay on the Amazon original series *Mozart in the Jungle*, a light and enjoyable little bauble (especially if you, like me, are a failed violinist who went to college next door to Oberlin Conservatory). The show is based on Blair Tindall's book of the same name, a memoir-cum-exposé of the classical music world, published, as it so happens, in 2005. Aaron

Bady, in noting the many ways the series departs from the source, says:

> Interspersed with her own memories and autobiography, her historical account of American classical music's rise and fall is relatively straightforward: like so many other apparently permanent features of American life (that are now in various states of free-fall and collapse), she argues, the midcentury boom in postwar government funding for arts and culture was a temporary and disastrous bubble. During that period of prosperity, many new groups were formed and American symphonies reached heights from which they could only fall and have fallen. She goes into great detail about how and why this happened—and places herself, a teenager in the 1970s, as one of the young musicians who got pulled in—but you can read the book if you want those details. For me, the interesting thing is the feeling of it: it feels right that her book was published in 2005, the same year as Tony Soprano's famous lament that he came in at the end, after the best was already over.

Now, I would be remiss if I didn't note that Tony Soprano, in fact, made that famous lament in the

Sopranos pilot in 1999, but I will not begrudge Bady his observation about America six years later, because it did feel like that. After the apparent, if unreal, if dangerous, martial unity of the immediate post-9/11 culture; after John Kerry windsurfed into electoral oblivion on the squalls of a lousy campaign, unable to respond to the evil insinuations of his rival; after, suddenly, it really did feel as if we'd tipped into a new century untethered in a lot of weird ways from the one immediately past, despite the fact that we were talking about mujahideen and Iran and all that *Reagan shit* all over again; I recall, in particular, a sense of real unmooredness, a drifting.

Chapter six, again. Months after John's death, Didion has taken up the crossword, something she "never before had the patience" to work on, "but now imagined…would encourage the return to constructive cognitive engagement." Seeing a clue that read "Sometimes you feel like…" she immediately thinks, "a motherless child." But there are only four spaces; the actual answer is "a nut."

I'm interested in how Didion, a product of the midcentury American boom as well as a chronicler of its false promises and inexorable dissolution and decline, could have produced a book so suited to the exact moment, "after the best was already over." The twenty-first century is an age of marvels, but it feels eerily as if something irreproducible has been lost. It's popular to imagine that the hinge on which the twentieth century pivoted to the twenty-first was September 11, 2001, but I'm of the opinion that the old era passed—and I say this with full awareness of just how artificial, how absurd the idea of a "century" is—several years later. *The Year of Magical Thinking* is not a political book, and yet note how it represents in a sense a full stop on the part of Joan Didion: "This year for the first time since I was twenty-nine I realized that my image of myself was of someone significantly younger."

Here's another scene from *The Sopranos*. Tony tells Christopher, his nephew, that he's "gonna take this family into the twenty-first century," to which Christopher replies, "We're already in the twenty-first century, though, T." Tony looks either annoyed or confused.

CHAPTER 20

τετέλεσται

I've never particularly cared for *Fresh Air* or the interviewing style of Terry Gross, whose verbal tics—the "likes," the stammers—always seem to me a very deliberate, very affected attempt to emulate precisely those characteristics—"so physically small, so temperamentally unobtrusive, and so neurotically inarticulate"—that Joan Didion had, very many years earlier, identified as the underlying secret of the success of her reporting. But you can't deny that Gross and her producers get the good guests, and they get them early.

Gross interviewed Didion about *The Year of Magical Thinking* on October 13, not even two weeks after the book's official publication date. It is during this interview that Didion learns she's won the National Book Award. Near the end of the segment, Gross asks

Didion if she is "any more or less worried about your own death now," leading to this exchange:

> *Didion:* No, I'm not worried about my own death.
> I think I'm less worried.
> *Gross:* Why?
> *Didion:* One of the things that worries us about dying always is we're afraid we're leaving people behind, and they won't be able to take care of themselves; we have to take care of them. But in fact, you see, I'm not leaving anybody behind. This is an area we shouldn't get into, I think.

After which Joan Didion, the "cool customer," the manager, the woman whom David Thomson, in his *London Review of Books* review of *Where I Was From*, called "a tough old bird" who "could make it to ninety herself," breaks, ever so slightly, and requires a few minutes to gather her thoughts—the few minutes, ironically, during which Gross's producer gets the news of the award.

This is the dramatic heart of the interview, I suppose, as well as the surprise revelation, but as I listened to it, and as I read the transcript, I found that I kept returning to something Didion says earlier on. Remember, Quintana had died that summer, that

August, just before *The Year of Magical Thinking* came out. Gross brings this up. She is interested in how, as both a mother and a writer, Didion could "deal" with that. She wants to know how, and whether, Didion had to think about rewriting or updating the book. Didion replies that it never crossed her mind. Gross, a bit incredulous, asks, "It never crossed your mind?" And Joan Didion replies, "It never crossed my mind. No. It was finished."

Christian readers will pardon this Jewish writer being a little slow to figure out where I almost remembered the phrase from. It is, of course, from John 19:28–30 (New King James Version):

> After this, Jesus, knowing that all things were now accomplished, that the Scripture might be fulfilled, said, "I thirst!" Now a vessel full of sour wine was sitting there; and they filled a sponge with sour wine, put it on hyssop, and put it to His mouth. So when Jesus had received the sour wine, He said, "It is finished!" And bowing His head, He gave up His spirit.

I have a feeling Didion would rather be considered a "tough old bird" than rendered as some kind of Christlike martyr. The echo is surely a coincidence, but as I've elsewhere confessed, being a Jew by culture but an atheist by disbelief, I have an abiding faith in coincidences. Here, what's notable is that the phrase, "It is finished," actually occurs twice, because the Greek word, *tetelestai*, is alternately translated in the twenty-eighth verse as "all things were now accomplished."

Either is a good way to describe the feeling of finishing a book, and either is also a way to describe *any* death. It seems to me that Didion did, intentionally or not, mean more than just that the thing was already at the printer. To wit: the life, the marriage, and the book that was the marriage and the lives, were all closed.

"On Rosh Hashanah it is written, and on Yom Kippur it is sealed." Jews say this, part of the liturgical poem *Unetaneh Tokef* on the High Holy Days. The seal is the closing of the book of life, which contains divine, irrevocable judgments of who will live and who will die in the coming year, and which will not be reopened until the coming year. Written, and sealed.

"What gives those December days a year ago their sharper focus," Didion writes, "is their ending."

CHAPTER 21

A PARASCEVE AND A PREPARATION

*Natural men have conceived a twofold use of sleep;
that it is a refreshing of the body in this life; that
it is a preparing of the soul for the next; that it is a
feast, and it is the grace at that feast; that it is our
recreation and cheers us, and it is our catechism and
instructs us; we lie down in a hope that we shall rise
the stronger, and we lie down in a knowledge that we
may rise no more. Sleep is an opiate which gives us
rest, but such an opiate, as perchance, being under it,
we shall wake no more.*

—John Donne, *Devotions upon Emergent Occasions*

Such an opiate. The banal beginning of my brother's ineluctable decline is something that I have yet to get my head around. "How does 'flu' morph into whole-body infection?" John Gregory Dunne had asked.

"[He] had seemed fixed on this point…and had never received an answer he found satisfactory." In fact, my brother's story has lately become a headline, as the apparently endemic use of opiates among people who look like my brother (which is to say, other white people) has pushed the knotty questions of drug abuse and prohibition out of the decades-long script of war and incarceration.

I admit to having mixed feelings about this, firstly because I recognize the deep injustice of it, of needing a certain type of person to flip the character from perpetrator to victim, from criminal to patient, and secondly because I do not want to see his experience generalized. This is deeply irrational of me. I believe in the legalization of controlled substances. I believe cities and towns should follow the European model of providing safe, clean places for users to shoot up. I believe in recovery models that consider control and moderation of use to be just as legitimate as total abstinence. Yet it feels like the universality of the experience takes away Nathan's uniqueness, that it deprives us— his family, I mean: our mother, our father, and me—of the particularity of his life and of his death, that it represents a diminishing of our grief.

This, I think, was for me the most surprising thing about grief. Grief is a drug. There is a common misconception that the underlying pathology of drug use is some kind of pleasure principle, that to want to get high is to seek pleasure, euphoria, release. But equally at work is a need for an intensity of experience, sometimes deeply *unpleasant*. Sure, my friends and I smoked weed, which was fun, or did coke, which was sort of fun, or ate mushrooms, which was usually fun. But we also did AMT and DMT and DXM and ketamine—research chemicals, we called them—which, though they could occasionally be fun, far more often resulted in states of sheer terror and dissociative psychosis. If there was pleasure in it, it was the pleasure of extreme endurance or of sexual masochism. It was not, except in the most attenuated sense, about feeling *good*.

Grief is startling in its intensity, and it's hard to release in part because as soon as you feel it for the first time, you know that what beckons beyond when you come down from it is dull, yawning, numb. Grief is like all the drugs combined. You rush around performing aimless, obsessive tasks as if you're on speed; you dissociate and lose the threads of causality; you hallucinate impossible scenarios. Joan Didion imagined that John would walk back through the door and need his shoes.

I stood in the receiving line at Schugar's, the funeral home on Centre Avenue, before my brother's service, thinking somehow I was going to look up and find that the familiar hand I was blankly shaking as I muttered, "Thanks for coming" for the hundredth time belonged to him, that it was elaborately a joke, even though I had seen the ashes.

He was prescribed painkillers for his shattered and repaired leg. The dosage was too high, or maybe he overmedicated himself. Maybe he was less stoical than the face he'd presented to the world since his early adolescence and couldn't handle the pain—I've long suspected this to be the likely case. He was a functioning addict for what, another seven, eight years? He got by on charm and good looks, told the right lies, preserved the correct appearances, knew to present himself as rakishly dissolute, the sort of minor demerit and flaw that people forgive, frankly, in a good-looking white kid from a prosperous and well-connected family. He'd get it together one of these days, when he got sick of tending bar. Then he didn't. This is such an ordinary story. It has so little to commend it to anyone's interest except as another datum in the sociological narrative of the "opioid epidemic." If it shocked us when it all began to fall apart, it was only because we'd been blind, overconfident, concerned about the wrong things for the wrong reasons. In retrospect it isn't shocking. It isn't even surprising.

It was unique only in that he was my brother. He was Nate. "[T]he dust that is swirled into a shape / And crumbles and is swirled again had but one shape / That was this man." The peculiarity, the particularity, in each death is the person who dies. All of us die, but we are ourselves alone. In hating the cruel normalcy of the way my brother died, what I hate is the shadow it casts backward onto the life he lived. How silly and how unfair. But hating it is the last, lingering taste of the first hit of grieving, long after I grew tolerant of it and it lost its edge. I still find myself at the most unexpected moment thinking, *I can't fucking believe that's how he did it*. I get so angry again, if only for a short time.

CHAPTER 22

TOUGH ENOUGH

This book is for Robert Silvers. It is also for John Gregory Dunne, who lived through my discovering what he already knew.

—JOAN DIDION, *Political Fictions*

Midway through *The Year of Magical Thinking*, after Quintana has shown the first tentative signs of recovery from her second hospitalization, the decision is made to fly her from LA back to New York where she will do rehab. This involves an air ambulance, a flight on a little Cessna jet with barely enough room for the tiny Didion to squeeze in along with her daughter, the paramedics, and the pilots. They land at a little airstrip in Kansas to refuel halfway through the flight and send the kids who manage the strip out to grab some fast food for them while the plane fuels.

While we waited, the paramedics suggested that we take turns getting some exercise. When my turn came I stood frozen on the tarmac for a moment, ashamed to be free and outside when Quintana could not be, then walked to where the runway ended and the corn started. There was a little rain and unstable air and I imagined a tornado coming. Quintana and I were Dorothy. We were both free. In fact we were out of here.

After thinking of *The Wizard of Oz*, she thinks of *Nothing Lost*, Dunne's final novel, which was in galleys—typically, the final stage of editing for a novel—when he died. Dunne had written a passage with a tornado.

For me, though, the moment at the airstrip is an uncanny echo of "Insider Baseball," an essay in *Political Fictions*.

About this baseball on the tarmac. On the day that Michael Dukakis appeared at the high school in Woodland Hills and at the office plaza in San Diego and in the schoolyard in San Jose, there was, although it did not appear on the schedule, a fourth event, what was referred to among the television crews as "a tarmac arrival with ball tossing." This event had taken place in late morning, on the tarmac at the San Diego airport, just after the campaign's chartered 737 had rolled to a stop and the candidate had emerged. There had been a moment of hesitation, or decision. Then baseball mitts had been produced, and Jack Weeks, the traveling press secretary, had tossed a ball to the candidate. The candidate had tossed the ball back. The rest of us had stood in the sun and given this our full attention: some forty adults standing on a tarmac watching a diminutive figure in shirtsleeves and a red tie toss a ball, undeflected even by the arrival of an Alaska Airlines 767, to his press secretary.

"Just a regular guy," one of the cameramen had said, his inflection that of the "union official" who confided, in an early Dukakis commercial aimed at blue-collar voters, that he had known "Mike" a long time, and backed him despite his not being "your shot-and-beer kind of guy."

She goes on to document the way reporters for CNN and *U.S. News and World Report* and the *Washington Post* wrote or described this moment of deliberate artifice as if it were a spontaneous, natural occurrence. Then: "What we had in the tarmac arrival with ball tossing, then, was an understanding: a repeated moment witnessed by many people, all of whom believed it to be a setup and yet most of whom believed that only an outsider, only someone too 'naïve' to know the rules of the game, would so describe it."

It's a masterful moment of anti–political journalism, or perhaps political antijournalism, because, as she did way back in '68, she insinuated herself into a scene by being unobtrusive and reported back how everyone behaved when they thought they were among only themselves. She exposed the unsubtle fakery of a professional con: "The narrative is made up of many such understandings, tacit agreements, small and large, to overlook the observable in the interests of obtaining a dramatic story line."

Ironically—I am sure the irony was not lost on her when she wrote it—Didion catches herself in the same trap in *The Year of Magical Thinking*: "That night when we arrived at the Rusk Institute Gerry and Tony were waiting outside to meet the ambulance. Gerry asked how the flight had been. I said that we had shared a Big Mac in a cornfield in Kansas. 'It wasn't a Big Mac,' Quintana said. 'It was a Quarter Pounder.'"

What narrative was she trying to impose? I can easily imagine: the fraught but heroic flight back east, the dramatic but humorous stopover in Kansas, the Big Mac the precise detail that makes it a *story*, and in making it a story, obliging it to follow the narrative rules that require a resolution. But there are no resolutions.

There is always a tarmac. When we were boys, Dad used to take Nate and me to the Latrobe Airport every year for the Westmoreland County Air Show. We'd wander the runways and tarmacs looking at vintage planes and climbing into the cockpit of World War II–era bombers and watching the stunt planes and eating Italian ice. There was usually a show by the Blue Angels or the Thunderbirds. Some years we'd take my grandmother, Lena; Lena loves airplanes.

I recall, although I have no specific memory of his ever actually saying it, that this younger version of my brother had at some point expressed a desire to be a fighter pilot. I remember it because I had recently gotten glasses—I must have been in fifth or sixth grade at the time—and Nate informed me that you couldn't be a fighter pilot or astronaut if you had to wear glasses. I'd also recently had braces; maybe I still had braces. It was not, you can imagine, the best time of my life. I remember we saw the B-2 stealth bomber do a flyover. I remember Nate had the terrible bowl haircut that was popular at the time, and his ears still stuck straight out. (He was vain about his ears. He would as a teenager beg to have a minor cosmetic procedure—a sliver of skin and cartilage removed from behind each ear so that it lay more normally against his head—which, after arguing, our parents gave him.)

Another time. Also at the Latrobe Airport. For Christmas, Dad chartered us a sightseeing flight, a little four-seat, single-engine propeller plane. The flight took us to Pittsburgh, looped a few times around downtown, and then returned to the airport—an hour or two overall. Neither Nate nor I had ever been in a propeller plane before. When we were over the city, I turned to show Nate that I'd spotted Three Rivers Stadium, but he was asleep. He slept nearly the whole time.

We had cornfields, too. After we moved to Uniontown, after our parents built the four-bedroom colonial on Saratoga Drive in Heritage Hills, we used to go over the wire fence behind Tyler Calabrese's house into a cornfield. It was feed corn, and we'd steal ears of it to strip off their kernels in order to thrown the corn at houses in the neighborhood. I don't ever remember actually corning any houses, but I do remember that if you weren't careful, you could rub the skin right off your thumb when you were stripping away the hard little grains from the cob.

"It had seemed to me," Didion writes, "on the day in Quintana's room at Presbyterian when I read the final proof for *Nothing Lost* that there might be a grammatical error in the last sentence of the passage about J.J. McClure and Teresa Kean and the tornado." She considers whether or not to correct it, but the idea paralyzes her. "How had he written it? What did he have in mind? How would he want it?" Ultimately, she decides to leave it as it is: "The error, if it was an error, had been there from the beginning. I left it as it was."

I was surprised to find in this passage an echo of a brief passage from a Jack London novel that she'd cited in *Where I Was From*. London and his wife Charmian (whom he called Wolf-Mate!) were cranks, to say the least, earnest believers in an agrarian-arcadian vision that neither of them had the wherewithal or skills to instantiate—making them therefore, in Didion's telling, fairly perfect human metaphors for California writ large. They were also utterly devoted to each other; Charmian remained a believer in Jack's agricultural experiments even after utter failure. She defended him in strident letters even after he'd died. Didion cites one:

> Just three weeks before this letter was written, Jack London had died, at forty, of uremic poisoning and one final, fatal dose of the morphine prescribed to calm his renal colic. In the last novel he was to write, *The Little Lady of the Big House*, he had allowed his protagonist and author-surrogate to ask these questions, a flash of the endemic empty in a work that is otherwise a fantasy of worldly and social success: "Why? What for? What's it worth? What's it all about?"

Back on the tarmac in San Diego, according to Mike Kramer's narration in *U.S. News and World Report*, he asks, "tongue-in-cheek," what playing a game of catch in hundred-degree heat says about candidate Dukakis's "mental stability." "What it means," says the candidate, "is that I'm tough."

CHAPTER 23

AS WITH A FLOOD

Later in Ariès's *Western Attitudes toward Death*, in discussing the extravagance of nineteenth-century mourning, *hysterical mourning*, Ariès notes in passing an 1893 story by Mark Twain, entitled—I find it hard to imagine this mere coincidence, but it must be—"The Californian's Tale." This is also—again, an odd coincidence—the moment when Ariès identifies a significant change in the sensations of grief and the practice of mourning: "Henceforth, and this is a very important change, the death which is feared is no longer so much the death of the self as the death of another, *la morte de toi*, thy death."

All Ariès notes about the Twain story is that it deals with a man who after nineteen years fails to accept that his wife is dead and each year, on the anniversary of her death or disappearance, awaits "her impossible return in the company of sympathetic friends who helped him maintain his illusion." It's a fair summary, although it doesn't quite do justice to the particular dark humor of the story. Twain's unnamed narrator encounters this deranged widower after wandering through a lovingly described but utterly forlorn and abandoned California countryside full of ruined homesteads and towns gone back to the earth. Twain deliberately writes in a tone suggesting a ghost story—it has a hint of Poe to it; since Twain by his own estimation found Poe unreadable, there might even be an element of intentional parody. The end turns more classically Twain. He's led you almost to believe the wife, or the ghost of the wife, may yet appear. But it turns out that some seemingly sympathetic friends, who at first seemed to have come over also to await the wife's return, actually intend to get the husband drunk, to drug him to sleep. They tell the narrator the widower will forget it in the morning anyway, and it'll all be calm until the same time rolls around next year.

There's a passage in the story that seems to me to express precisely the odd feeling of writing a book about mourning, a book about grief, a book about the dead. The narrator has been allowed into a bedroom to wash his hands. He continuously notes how neat and well decorated and homey it is, as compared to "long weeks of daily and nightly familiarity with miners' cabins—with all which this implies of dirt floor, never-made beds, tin plates and cups, bacon and beans and black coffee, and nothing of ornament but war pictures from the Eastern illustrated papers tacked to the log walls."

By this time I was wiping my hands and glancing from detail to detail of the room's belongings, as one is apt to do when he is in a new place, where everything he sees is a comfort to his eye and his spirit; and I became conscious, in one of those unaccountable ways, you know, that there was something there somewhere that the man wanted me to discover for myself. I knew it perfectly, and I knew he was trying to help me by furtive indications with his eye, so I tried hard to get on the right track, being eager to gratify him. I failed several times, as I could see out of the corner of my eye without being told; but at last I knew I must be looking straight at the thing—knew it from the pleasure issuing in invisible waves from him. He broke into a happy laugh, and rubbed his hands together, and cried out:

"That's it! You've found it. I knew you would. It's her picture."

This is to say: to write about grief is to find yourself trying to direct some nameless reader "by furtive indications" to discover the picture you'd placed in the room expressly to be discovered.

"I did not want to finish the year," Didion writes, "because I know that as the days pass, as January becomes February and February becomes summer, certain things will happen. My image of John at the instant of his death will become less immediate, less raw." It is true. The image of the dead, alive, will "become more remote, even 'mudgy,' softened, transmuted into whatever best serves my life without him." But it is also and paradoxically true that our dead become, as did the dead wife in Twain's story, their own picture in a "daguerreotype-case," a thing preserved as a fixed, still image that cannot be a life.

It has been more than eight years since my brother died. If after a year or two I found myself thinking of him less than I had thought of him immediately afterward, then now I discover that I think of him more often, that I speak of him more often. But I may *remember* him less, and when I do, I find it hard not to see him only as a few particular and iconic photographs of him: the picture of the two of us as a baby and a toddler, where I'm wearing a shirt that says, "I'm the big brother"; the picture of him, obscured by goggles and gear, on a snowboard midair from one winter when he went to a snowboarding camp out west; the picture of him, me, and our mother on Muir Beach in California, the year we all spent Thanksgiving in San Francisco.

That year, after a few days in the city, we drove up to Napa. I remember Mom telling Dad not to take the switchbacks so fast on whatever tiny road we took over the hills to Sonoma that evening, and I remember my dad asking me, as we passed a team of Lycra-clad cyclists doing a pretty good cadence up the hill we were descending, if I'd be nuts enough to ride a hill like that. I'd just started cycling as a more serious fitness pursuit. I said yes, thought *probably not*. We stayed a couple of nights at an inn near the Russian River, and since the inn had a good restaurant, and since this was just before the universal availability of GPS, when it was a pain in the ass to navigate around the dark country at night, we ate dinner both nights at the inn. There was a courtyard and a big tree, and although the inn was lit up, it was still darker than the city. After dinner on the second night, I went out with Nate to smoke a cigarette. I wasn't really a smoker, but after three or so bottles of wine between the five of us—Nate's girlfriend at the time was with us too—it didn't take much to convince me to have a smoke.

For all his pretense of cool, for his magnetism and superficial confidence, my brother was a provincial kid at heart. He'd have never admitted it, but he took to Uniontown, the little seat of Fayette County where I'd only spent my adolescence but where he had well and truly grown up, in a way that neither I nor my parents ever did. Even Pittsburgh was sometimes a little much for him. I don't think, for instance, that he ever once took a bus. He never walked anywhere. That night— it was our last night in Sonoma before returning to San Francisco for a day and then flying home—he confessed to me that he'd been bored on the trip. He liked wine just fine, but the endless prattle at the wineries we visited annoyed him, and he figured a vineyard was just an especially monotonous farm. And he and his girlfriend had hardly seen San Francisco, except when they'd come with me and Mom and Dad for a few obligatory tourist trips to see sea lions, to ride a cable car. He was afraid to wander around, though he'd have denied it. Afraid to get lost. Afraid, perhaps, to seem foolish. (That is one thing I've learned traveling over the years: You inevitably seem foolish. It's best not to worry about it.) He'd preferred to drink at the hotel bar, which was, admittedly, a very nice hotel bar, but still. I'd invited him to come with me one night to visit some old college friends of mine in the city; he'd declined. I think he was scared to take public transit, and I was too cheap to take a cab.

So he'd been bored on the trip, although I will say this of his courage: he was the only one of us willing to take off his shoes and roll his pants to the knees and stroll out into the freezing Pacific in November for twenty or thirty seconds before running back to shore. I told him I'd enjoyed it, and he rolled his eyes and said that's because I was gay and boring, the former of which was certainly, the latter probably, true. You're getting to be like Mom and Dad, he said. That was also probably true. We smoked, and then we saw a shooting star cross the sky above California. I had never seen one, have never seen one since. That was cool, Nate said. For some reason, we both found this very funny.

In "Narcissus," Delmore Schwartz writes:

Dusk we are, to dusk returning, after the burbing,
After the gold fall, the fallen ash, the bronze,

Scattered and rotten, after the white null
   statues which
Are winter, sleep, and nothingness: when
Will the houselights of the universe
Light up and blaze?
      For it is not the sea
Which murmurs in a shell,
And it is not only heart, at harp o'clock,
It is the dread terror of the uncontrollable
Horses of the apocalypse, running in wild dread
Toward Arcturus—and returning as suddenly…

I do not believe in God or any sort of afterlife, and the shooting star is just a mass of rock and iron burning in the atmosphere as it falls, but there is yet the moment when you see it and think it's the landing light of an aircraft before you realize that it's flown too fast and flashed too brightly for that, and recognizing what it is, you remember that there's something—an infinity of somethings—beyond this one world after all.